DEDICATION

To Silence — my first teacher.

To every seeker who has walked through confusion, chaos, and noise — and still chosen clarity.

To the timeless rhythm of Dharma that beats quietly beneath every moment,
And To Those Who Listen Closely Enough To Hear It.

To **Sri Aadi Shankar Acharya, Sri Bhagavan Ramana Maharshi, Nisargadatta Maharaj, Osho, Jiddu Krishna Murthy,**

ACKNOWLEDGMENTS

This book was not written alone — it was lived, questioned, and discovered through the many minds and hearts that crossed my path.

To my **family**, who gave me the space to think deeply, speak slowly, and live truthfully — your patience has been my sanctuary.

To my **teachers and mentors**, visible and invisible, who opened the doors of both **Sociology and Vedānta**, showing that wisdom and inquiry are not opposites but partners.

To the **millennials and Gen Z dreamers** I've met through talks, classrooms, and workshops — you are the real inspiration behind these pages. Your restlessness is sacred fuel; may it always lead you home.

To the **timeless sages** — from the Gītā to the Upaniṣads, from Buddha to Bodhidharma — your silence still teaches. This work merely translates your grace for a hurried generation.

To **my friends and readers**, who believed in this idea when it was only a whisper: thank you for helping me build it into a rhythm that could be shared.

And finally, to **Life itself** — for every uncertainty, every pause, and every dawn that whispered:

"Stay steady. You are the sky, not the storm."

TABLE OF CONTENTS

PART II · THE INNER SCIENCE OF STEADINESS

PART III · THE OUTER SCIENCE OF ORDER

INTRODUCTION

The Forgotten Discipline

We live in an age of endless beginnings — new goals, new apps, new habits — and yet, few completions. Everyone wants transformation, but few can stay with the process long enough for transformation to happen.

In this restless age, *consistency* has become a forgotten virtue.We chase intensity — the perfect morning routine, the 10x plan, the dopamine rush of progress — but the universe itself doesn't rush. The sunrise doesn't skip a day. The tide never forgets its rhythm.
The ancients called this rhythm **Ṛta** — the cosmic order. It is the invisible consistency that holds the stars in their paths, the seasons in their sequence, and the human mind in balance.

Somewhere between our smartphones and our short attention spans, we lost this rhythm.
We became addicted to *newness* and allergic to *discipline*.But long before modern productivity gurus wrote about habits and systems, India's sages had already discovered the secret:

The steady mind is the liberated mind.

They called this steadiness *Dharma* — the art of acting rightly, repeatedly, and consciously.
They called its fruit *Karma* — the ripple effect of every consistent choice.
And they called its goal *Moksha* — the freedom that comes not from doing more, but from doing what matters, again and again, with awareness.

This book is not about working harder.
It's about *working in rhythm* — aligning your daily life with the deeper order that already sustains everything.

It is a bridge between the silence of the Upanishads and the noise of your notifications, between the discipline of the Gita and the distractions of your inbox.

Each chapter draws from an eternal scripture and translates its wisdom into modern clarity — how to be focused like Arjuna in chaos, patient like Rama in duty, and free like a sage in the middle of a storm.

Because consistency isn't just about success — it's about becoming *unshakable.*
When your inner rhythm matches the rhythm of life itself, nothing can pull you off balance — not failure, not fear, not even time.

You don't need more motivation.
You need alignment.
You need rhythm.
You need to remember what the ancients never forgot —
that consistency is the modern form of spirituality.

Welcome to **Unshakable** — a journey through timeless order in a distracted age.

Preface

The Search for Steadiness

In every age, people have chased change — faster growth, higher success, louder validation.But the quiet ones have always known the secret: ***progress without peace is only motion.***This book is a bridge between the stillness of ancient India and the stimulation of modern life.It was written not to preach, but to practice — to remind us that beneath every breath,there is a rhythm waiting to be remembered: the rhythm of Dharma.

Chapter 1

Ṛta 2.0: Living in Tune with the Universal Order

The Rhythm We Forgot

Every morning, millions of us wake up to an alarm that interrupts sleep rather than welcomes dawn.We scroll through headlines before we stretch, check notifications before we breathe, and eat breakfast while reading emails.By the time the day truly begins, our *inner rhythm* is already hijacked by ***outer urgency.***

We have never been more connected — yet never more disordered.
Our bodies live in daylight, but our minds wander in chaos.

The ancients would have called this **"A-Rita"** — life disconnected from the *order of things.*

The Sacred Law of Ṛta

Before there were religions, there was **Ṛta (ऋत)** — the invisible harmony that holds the cosmos together.

Ṛta is the law that makes rivers flow, stars rise, and hearts beat in sequence.

It is the **first form of consistency** — divine regularity expressed through creation.

ऋतं च सत्यं चाभीद्धात् तपसोऽध्यजायत।

ṛtaṃ ca satyaṃ cābhīd dhāt tapaso 'dhyajāyata

(Rig Veda 10.190.1)

Translation:

"From the discipline of Tapas (focused austerity), were born Ṛta (cosmic order) and Satya (truth)."

Commentary:

This is one of the earliest declarations of the human relationship with consistency.

The universe did not arise from chance — it was born from *Tapas*, disciplined energy.

Ṛta is not control; it is *commitment.*

It is what happens when divine energy stays consistent enough to become creation.

In modern language — **Consistency is the architecture of existence.**

The Steady Sun and the Dancing Earth

The Vedas remind us that even gods follow Ṛta.

The sun, the wind, the seasons — all act within rhythm.

सूर्यो ऋतस्य प्रतिमानमस्तु।

sūryo ṛtasya pratimānam astu

(Rig Veda 1.115.1)

Translation:

“The Sun is the visible embodiment of Ṛta.”

Commentary:

The sun rises and sets without pride or delay — steady, impartial, luminous.

It gives warmth not because it chooses to, but because it *is its Dharma to do so.*

Consistency, in this sense, is not mechanical — it is *devotional.*
The sun does not tire of rising; it fulfills its order in silence.

"He who moves according to Ṛta, upholds the world."

(Rig Veda 5.63.7)

In your own life, you are the sun of your small universe.
When your actions are steady and pure, everything around you aligns — work, energy, relationships, health.
When you act erratically, your orbit collapses.

Ṛta and Modern Disorder

Science today speaks of **circadian rhythm**, **neural homeostasis**, and **flow cycles.**
All these modern discoveries echo the same truth:
Your biology is anciently wired to the order of the universe.

When you sleep, eat, and act in sync with that order — health flourishes.
When you resist it — anxiety, fatigue, and confusion follow.

ऋतेन भूमिः प्रतिष्ठिता।

ṛtena bhūmiḥ pratiṣṭhitā

(Atharva Veda 12.1.12)

Translation:

"By Ṛta, the Earth stands firm."

Just as the earth stays firm through order, so does your life through *discipline.*
Your consistency stabilizes your inner world the way gravity stabilizes planets.

Modern Application — Practicing Ṛta Today

Here's how to live Ṛta in a 21st-century lifestyle:

1. Honor the Dawn (Udaya Kriya)

उत्तिष्ठत जाग्रत प्राप्य वरान् निबोधत।

uttishthata jāgrata prāpya varān nibodhata
(Katha Upanishad 1.3.14)

"Arise, Awake, and learn from the wise."

The Upanishadic call is not just physical — it's spiritual.
To rise before the world rises is to align with the first rhythm of the day.
Your first thought shapes the rest.

Practice:

- Wake during *Brahma Muhurta* (before sunrise).
- Sit in silence for two minutes before touching your phone.
- Observe your breath — the simplest proof of Ṛta within you.

---

2. Make Time a Circle, Not a Race

Time was cyclical in Vedic thought, not linear.

Ṛta means returning daily to what is essential — prayer, work, rest, reflection.

“कालः कर्षति भूतानि सर्वाण्याप्यययत्यपि।”

Time draws all beings onward and brings them to rest again.
(Mahabharata, Shanti Parva 232.9)

Practice:
Don’t chase time; revolve with it.
Work and rest in fixed rhythms.
Consistency builds serenity because it ends decision fatigue.

---

3. Transform Routine into Ritual

तपसा जायते तेजः।

"From discipline arises radiance."
(Atharva Veda 11.5.18)

Every small act done with awareness becomes sacred.
Cooking, writing, walking — when repeated consciously, they create order in mind and matter.
This is *karma as meditation.*

Practice:
Pick one act — your tea, your journaling, your evening walk — and treat it as a sacred vow of steadiness.

In that act, find your daily Ṛta.

The Science of Ṛta

Modern research echoes Vedic insight:

- **Circadian Alignment:** Regular sleep and meal times restore hormonal balance.
- **Flow Psychology:** Regular creative work builds "effortless focus."

- **Habit Loop Theory:** Consistency reduces cognitive load — freeing willpower for creativity.

The sages intuitively knew what science now proves:

Consistency is the mother of clarity.

The Inner Ṛta — Mental and Emotional Order

Ṛta is not only external order — it is *internal stability.*

Emotional consistency is the subtler form of cosmic balance.

When you react differently every day — kind one moment, harsh the next — your mind loses *ṛta*, your inner rhythm.

Meditation restores that pulse.

चित्तं यदा निरुद्धं योगोऽथ भवति।

"When the mind becomes steady, Yoga arises."
(Yoga Sutra 1.2)

Stillness is not absence of thought; it is the alignment of thought with purpose.

The Universal Symphony

When the Rig Veda describes the universe, it often uses the word **"ṛtam bṛhatam"** — *the vast order.*

Everything, from the smallest atom to the largest galaxy, hums in that vastness.

ऋतेन देवाः पतिरो नृमणा अनु।

"By Ṛta the gods, ancestors, and humans are sustained."

(Rig Veda 1.164.42)

You are not separate from that cosmic rhythm — you *are* part of it.
To live in harmony with it is to rediscover your natural consistency.

Closing Reflection

When you feel lost, don't seek more motivation — seek rhythm.
When you feel restless, don't add more tasks — remove disorder.
When you feel empty, don't chase stimulation — restore silence.

Consistency is not about perfection; it is about *participation in Ṛta.*

सत्येनोत्तभिता भूमिः सूर्येण तपसा धृतः।

"The Earth is upheld by Truth, the Sun by steadfast discipline."
(Atharva Veda 12.1.1)

Let your life become like the sun —
rising without hesitation,
shining without pride,
and resting without guilt.

That is Ṛta in practice.

That is the first step toward being *Unshakable.*

Chapter 2

The Dharma Algorithm: Purpose Beyond Preference

Part I—The Bhagavad Gītā Lens

When Arjuna dropped his bow on Kurukṣetra, he wasn't merely paralysed by emotion—he faced the same confusion every modern soul meets daily:

What should I do when my feelings resist my purpose?

1□□ कर्मण्येवाधिकारस्ते मा फलेषु कदाचन

karmaṇy evādhikāras te mā phaleṣu kadācana – *BG 2.47*

"Your right is to the action alone, never to its fruits."

Consistency begins where preference ends.
The Gītā teaches that steady action—detached from reward—is the highest intelligence.
Modern relevance: show up for the process, not the applause.

2□□ समत्वं योग उच्यते – BG 2.48

"Evenness of mind is called Yoga."
Emotional steadiness is not coldness; it is *available focus.*
The leader, parent, or creator who acts from calm continuity becomes unshakable.

3□□ श्रेयान् स्वधर्मो विगुणः – BG 3.35

"Better one's own duty though imperfectly done than another's well performed."

Purpose is personal algorithm; copying others causes existential bugs.

4□□ नयितं कुरु कर्म त्वं – BG 3.8

"Perform your bounden duty; action is superior to inaction."
Avoiding decisions is also a decision—the wrong one.

Discipline sustains flow; procrastination breaks Ṛta.

5□□ योगस्थः कुरु कर्माणि – BG 2.48

"Established in Yoga, perform action."
Work from centeredness, not restlessness. The true performer is inwardly still.

6□□ तस्मात् सर्वेषु कालेषु मामनुस्मर युध्य च – BG 8.7

"Therefore, remember Me at all times and fight."
Spiritual mindfulness does not avoid the battlefield; it refines participation.
Today's battlefields are emails, exams, deadlines—fight with awareness.

7□□ उद्धरेदात्मनाऽऽत्मानं – BG 6.5

"Let a man lift himself by his own Self."
No external push substitutes internal recall.
Self-responsibility is the first rule in the Dharma Algorithm.

8□☐ न हि कश्चित्क्षणमपि जातु तिष्ठत्यकर्मकृत् – **BG 3.5**

"No one can remain actionless even for a moment."
Movement is built into existence; consistency simply aligns it.

9□☐ स्वभावजेन कौन्तेय निबद्धः स्वेन कर्मणा – **BG 18.60**

"You are bound to act by your own nature."
Recognise your inherent design; purpose is coded in temperament.

10 यत् करोषि यदश्नासि… तत्कुरुष्व मदर्पणम् – **BG 9.27**

"Whatever you do, do it as an offering to Me."
When every act is offering, motivation becomes sacred energy.

11□☐ उद्योगिनं पुरुषसिंहमुपैति लक्ष्मीः – **(derived from BG 6 ethos)**

Consistency attracts grace (*Lakṣmī*). Effort invites fortune; wishful thinking repels it.

12□☐ योगो योगात्मतां वहति – **BG 6.46-47 theme**

True Yogi = Consistent Karma + Inner Bhakti + Clear Jñāna.
Balance of head, hand, and heart—Gītā's tri-code.

13□☐ श्रद्धावान् लभते ज्ञानम् – BG 4.39

"The faithful attain wisdom."

Faith = long-term consistency of attention.

14□☐ अनन्याश्चिन्तयन्तो मां – BG 9.22

"Those who think of Me single-mindedly, I carry their needs."

Focused devotion stabilises the wandering algorithm called mind.

15□☐ स्वधर्मे निधनं श्रेयः – BG 3.35 refrain

Dying in one's Dharma is better than living in borrowed passion.

In a career or calling, authenticity is sustainability.

Modern Integration

The "Dharma Algorithm" is the code of meaningful consistency:

1. **Input:** Self-knowledge (Swadharma)
2. **Process:** Detachment from results
3. **Loop:** Daily disciplined action
4. **Output:** Peace, not burnout

When purpose drives action, results follow automatically—just as gravity follows mass.

Arjuna's paralysis mirrors our daily indecision between *what*

feels good and *what is right.*
The Gītā's answer: act rightly, steadily, and leave outcomes to cosmic computation.

Part II —The Rāmāyaṇa Lens

If the Gītā teaches the *philosophy* of consistency, the Rāmāyaṇa shows its *practice.*
Rāma never preached Dharma—he lived it, step by measured step.

1□□ रामो विग्रहवान् धर्मः – (Valmiki Rāmāyaṇa Ayodhyā Kāṇḍa 1.18)

"Rāma is Dharma embodied."
He is not described as perfect because he never erred, but because he stayed steady through every error.

2□□ पितुर्वचनं सत्यं – Ayodhyā Kāṇḍa 33.19

"My father's word is truth."
Rāma's exile is the triumph of principle over comfort.
Modern echo: keep promises when no one watches.

3□☐ नात्यश्नतस्तु योगोऽस्ति – **echoed ethos; discipline in moderation**

Rāma's forest life mirrors balance—minimalism without resentment.

4□☐ सुखदुःखे समे कृत्वा – **parallel to BG 2.38**

When joy and sorrow were equal in his gaze, he personified equanimity.

5□☐ रामो दशरथात्मजः सत्यपराक्रमः – **Ayodhyā Kāṇḍa 1.10**

Truthful in valor—steadfast even when victory required pain.

6□☐ मृदुर् दाक्षिण्य संयुक्तः – **Ayodhyā Kāṇḍa 1.18**

Gentle yet firm—consistency of character amid shifting roles.

7□☐ न च रामः प्रतिकूलं कञ्चिदाचरति – **Ayodhyā Kāṇḍa 1.16**

He never acted contrary to Dharma.
Modern relevance: integrity = doing the same right thing under pressure.

8□☐ सीता पतिव्रता धर्मे स्थिताऽभवत् – **Araṇya Kāṇḍa**

Sītā's devotion shows emotional consistency—love as vow, not mood.

9□□ लक्ष्मणः नित्ययुक्तः – **Ayodhyā Kāṇḍa 1.21**

Lakṣmaṇa's service reflects disciplined support; loyalty as daily habit.

10□□ भरतः राज्यम् न इच्छति – **Ayodhyā Kāṇḍa 103.8**

Renouncing the throne for truth—consistency of values over opportunity.

11□□ हनुमान् रामकार्ये निरतः – **Sundara Kāṇḍa 1.23**

Hanumān, symbol of tireless focus: purpose made muscle.
He never asks, "What do I get?"—only, "What must be done?"

12□□ नान्यः पन्था अयनाय विद्यते – **Sundara Kāṇḍa 35.80**

"There is no other path for me."
Determination turns doubt into momentum.

13□□ रामो दृढव्रतः – **Ayodhyā Kāṇḍa 1.11**

"Rāma of firm vow."
Discipline as identity, not effort.

14□□ कायेन वाचा मनसा रामकार्ये – **Sundara Kāṇḍa 39.4**

"By body, speech, and mind, devoted to Rāma's work."
Total alignment—no internal civil war.

15□□ जयतिरामो धर्मेश्वरः – **Yuddha Kāṇḍa 128.21**

“Victory to Rāma, the Lord of Dharma.”

Consistency is victory itself; success merely follows.

Modern Commentary — Rāma as a Mirror

Each character in the Rāmāyaṇa reveals an algorithmic principle:

Archetype	Consistency Principle	Modern Equivalent
Rāma	Duty > Desire	Value-based leadership
Sītā	Devotion > Doubt	Emotional fidelity, patience
Lakṣmaṇa	Service > Self	Team consistency
Bharata	Renunciation > Recognition	Ethical governance

Hanumān	Focus > Fatigue	Peak performance mindset

The Rāmāyaṇa teaches that *Dharma is not convenience; it's commitment under contradiction.*
Every moral test is a stress-test of rhythm.

In workplaces, relationships, and nations, disorder begins when preference dethrones principle.
Rāma shows that consistency is not rigidity—it's intelligent alignment between **truth, action, and time.**

Closing Integration

Both scriptures run on the same code:

1. **Bhagavad Gītā = Inner Algorithm** — clarity of thought.
2. **Rāmāyaṇa = Outer Execution** — constancy in behavior.

Together they form the full stack of Dharma:

ज्ञानं कर्म च भक्तिच – Knowledge, Action, and Devotion in balance.

Modern life's noise can't delete this code; it only needs re-installation.

Every time you choose duty over distraction, principle over preference, patience over impulse—you debug your destiny.

"Be Rāma in conduct, Arjuna in action."

That is the Dharma Algorithm:

Chapter 3

The Battlefield Within: The Psychology of Constancy

1· The Modern Arjuna

Aarav sat before his laptop like a soldier before war.
Two job offers glowed on the screen—one stable but dull, the other exciting but uncertain.
His heart wanted one; his head feared it.
Messages buzzed, advice poured in, and he felt a quiet panic rising.
"Why," he wondered, "do I freeze whenever life asks for direction?"

The ancients called this moment **Arjuna's dilemma**.

Every human being eventually stands on **Kurukṣetra**, not a field of armies but the crossroads of conscience.
The true battle of life is not between people; it's between impulses within.

---

2 · Verse 1 —The Battle Is Inside

धर्मक्षेत्रे कुरुक्षेत्रे समवेता युयुत्सवः।

dharma-kṣetre kuru-kṣetre samavetā yuyutsavaḥ – Bhagavad Gītā 1.1

Translation: "On the field of Dharma, on the field of the Kurus, the warriors assembled, eager for battle."

Commentary:

The line appears geographical, yet *Dharma-kṣetra* lies within every mind where right and wrong wrestle.

Each day you enter this field—before decisions, conversations, even meals.

Practice: Pause before every major choice and ask: "Am I fighting for ego or for essence?"

---

3 · Verse 2 — When Doubt Paralyzes

क्लैब्यं मा स्म गमः पार्थ न एतत्त्वय्युपपद्यते।

klaibyaṁ mā sma gamaḥ pārtha na etattvayy upapadyate – BG 2.3

Translation: "Yield not to weakness, O Partha; it does not befit you."

Commentary:

Kṛṣṇa's first lesson isn't metaphysics—it's psychology.

He diagnoses emotional paralysis and prescribes courage.

Application: Name your hesitation aloud. Naming transforms fear from fog into form. Form can be faced.

---

4 · Verse 3 —The Science of Steady Mind

स्थितिप्रज्ञस्य का भाषा समाधिस्थिस्य केशव।

sthita-prajñasya kā bhāṣā samādhi-sthasya keśava – BG 2.54

Translation: "What is the mark of one whose wisdom is steady, O Kṛṣṇa?"

Commentary:

Arjuna asks the eternal question of psychology: "What does stability look like?"

Kṛṣṇa's answer (2.55): "When one gives up desires that disturb the mind, he becomes serene."

Practice: Before reacting, watch desire's direction—is it toward clarity or clutter?

---

5 · Verse 4 — Emotion as Energy

इन्द्रियाणि मनः बुद्धिरस्याधिष्ठानमुच्यते।

indriyāṇi manaḥ buddhir asyādhiṣṭhānam ucyate – *BG 3.40*

Translation: "Senses, mind, and intellect are said to be its seat."

Commentary:
Here "it" means *kāma*—desire.
Modern neuroscience agrees: stimuli → emotion → interpretation → action.
Traditional Insight: Restraint isn't suppression; it's redirection.
Turn emotion into motion—service, art, exercise, prayer.

---

6 · Verse 5 — Mind as Ally

उद्धरेदात्मनात्मानं नात्मानमवसादयेत्।

uddhared ātmanātmānaṁ nātmānam avasādayet – *BG 6.5*

Translation: "Lift yourself by yourself; let not yourself fall."

Commentary:
Self-help, Gītā-style: you are both doctor and patient.
No external savior replaces inner discipline.
Practice: When overwhelmed, repeat silently: "I can lift my own mind." Then breathe three slow cycles.

---

7 · Verse 6 — Habit as Destiny

अभ्यासेन तु कौन्तेय वैराग्येण च गृह्यते।

abhyāsena tu kaunteya vairāgyeṇa ca gṛhyate – BG 6.35

Translation: "By practice and detachment, O son of Kuntī, the mind is restrained."

Commentary:
Consistency = Abhyāsa + Vairāgya.
Practice builds momentum; detachment keeps balance.
Modern equation: Effort without expectation = Flow.

---

8 · Verse 7 — The Shadow Self

काम एष क्रोध एष रजोगुणसमुद्भवः।

kāma eṣa krodha eṣa rajo-guṇa-samudbhavaḥ – BG 3.37

Translation: "It is desire—born of passion—that becomes anger."

Commentary:

Frustrated desire mutates into aggression.

Seeing this chain early ends it.

Practice: Before reacting in anger, ask, "What was I wanting that I didn't get?" Clarity cools fire.

---

9 · Verse 8 — Witness Consciousness

यदा ते मोहकलिलं बुद्धिर्व्यतितरिष्यति।

yadā te moha-kalilaṁ buddhir vyatitariṣyati – BG 2.52

Translation: "When your intellect crosses the mire of delusion, you will stand as a witness."

Commentary:

Observation is liberation.

Modern mindfulness echoes the same: awareness without judgment ends inner war.
Exercise: Label thoughts as "seeing," "hearing," "worrying," instead of "I am worried." The seer returns to center.

---

10 · Verse 9 — From Reaction to Response

सुखदुःखे समे कृत्वा लाभालाभौ जयाजयौ।

sukha-duḥkhe same kṛtvā lābhā-lābhau jayā-jayau – BG 2.38

Translation: "Treat pleasure and pain, gain and loss, victory and defeat alike."

Commentary:
Equanimity is not apathy—it's accurate perception.
When events lose their label of "good/bad," energy returns to action.
Modern Application: Before checking social media or news, set intention: "I will see, not soak."

---

11 · Verse 10 — The Dharma of Decision

स्वधर्मे नधिनं श्रेयः परधर्मो भयावहः।

svadharme nidhanaṁ śreyaḥ para-dharmaḥ bhayāvahaḥ – BG 3.35

Translation: "Better to die in one's own dharma than to live another's."

Commentary:

Authenticity is the anchor of consistency.

The moment you imitate, you break rhythm with truth.

Exercise: List three activities that feel natural and three that feel forced. Build life around the first set.

---

12 · The Psychology Decoded

Inner Conflict	Dharma-Based Resolution
Doubt	Courage through clarity (BG 2.3)
Fear	Faith in Self (BG 6.5)
Distraction	Practice + Detachment (BG 6.35)
Anger	Awareness of Desire (BG 3.37)
Imitation	Authentic Duty (BG 3.35)

These are not commandments but cognitive therapies in poetic Sanskrit.

The Gītā was the world's first manual on emotional regulation.

---

13 · The Modern Battlefield Algorithm

Step 1 — Pause. Recognize the conflict.

Step 2 — Breathe. Three equal breaths return to center.

Step 3 — Name. Identify the emotion without judgment.

Step 4 — Discern. Ask "What is right by my nature, not just pleasant?"

Step 5 — Act. Do your duty without attachment to outcome.

Step 6 — Reflect. End each day reviewing not results but responses.

This is the **Dharma-decision algorithm**—ancient code for mental clarity.

---

14 · Arjuna in All of Us

Aarav finally chose—not the easier job, nor the riskier one, but the path aligned with his curiosity and conscience.
He said no to noise and yes to truth.

That moment, he realized Kṛṣṇa was never a person outside but a presence within—the steady voice beneath all voices.

---

15 · Closing Reflection

श्रेयान् स्वधर्मो विगुणः परधर्मात् स्वनुष्ठितात्।

śreyān svadharmo viguṇaḥ paradharmāt sv-anuṣṭhitāt – BG 18.47

Translation: "Better imperfectly to live one's own Dharma than perfectly another's."

Consistency is not robotic repetition; it's rhythmic honesty. When your outer action reflects your inner truth, mind and

Dharma synchronize—and the battlefield becomes a classroom. Victory, then, is not conquest but **constancy**.

Chapter 4

The Inner Battlefield: The Gītā on Daily Discipline

1 · A Morning War

Arun wakes at six, checks his phone, scrolls news, loses thirty minutes, then rushes through meditation half-heartedly.
By noon he's exhausted though he has barely acted.
Nothing external attacked him—the enemy was inner inertia, a subtle Kurukṣetra within.

The *Bhagavad Gītā* calls this the real war: **the daily conflict between clarity and craving.**

---

2 · Crisis of Will

क्लैब्यं मा स्म गमः पार्थ नैतत्त्वय्युपपद्यते।

क्षुद्रं हृदयदौर्बल्यं त्यक्त्वोत्तिष्ठ परन्तप॥

klaibyaṁ mā sma gamaḥ pārtha naitat tvayy upapadyate |

kṣudraṁ hṛdaya-daurbalyaṁ tyaktvottiṣṭha parantapa || – BG 2.3

Translation:
"Yield not to weakness, O Arjuna; such faintheartedness does not befit you. Cast off this petty weakness of heart and rise!"

Commentary:
Every dawn carries the same call: *Rise again.* Procrastination is modern faintheartedness. Discipline begins the moment we refuse the first excuse.

---

3 · Purpose over Emotion

कर्मण्येवाधिकारस्ते मा फलेषु कदाचन ॥ – **BG 2.47**

"Your right is to action alone, never to its fruits."

Consistency means doing today's right action without demanding today's reward. Each completed task is a brick in invisible architecture.

---

4 · Equanimity: Emotional Stability as Skill

योगस्थः कुरु कर्माणि सङ्गं त्यक्त्वा धनञ्जय।

सिद्ध्यसिद्ध्योः समो भूत्वा समत्वं योग उच्यते॥ – **BG 2.48**

“Perform duty established in balance, abandoning attachment; evenness of mind is called Yoga.”

Commentary:
Modern translation: *Do your work, keep your cool.* Emails, markets, moods fluctuate—discipline is staying steady when results swing.

---

5 · The Steady Mind

यदा ते मोहकलिलं बुद्धिर्व्यतितरिष्यति।

तदा गन्तासि निर्वेदं श्रोतव्यस्य श्रुतस्य च॥ – **BG 2.52**

“When your intellect crosses the forest of delusion, you become indifferent to what is yet to be heard or has been heard.”

Commentary:
Information overload is our forest. Consistency grows when attention is reclaimed from excess input.

---

6 · Action as Prayer

यत्करोषि यदश्नासि यज्जुहोषि ददासि यत्।

यत्तपस्यसि कौन्तेय तत्कुरुष्व मदर्पणम्॥ – BG 9.27

"Whatever you do, eat, offer, or give—do it as an offering to Me."

Transform chores into consecrations. When routine becomes ritual, fatigue disappears; the act gains sacred momentum.

---

7 · Self-Mastery over Self-Indulgence

उद्धरेदात्मनाऽऽत्मानं नात्मानमवसादयेत्।

आत्मैव ह्यात्मनो बन्धुरात्मैव रिपुरात्मनः॥ – BG 6.5

"Let a man lift himself by his Self; the Self alone is his friend or his enemy."

Commentary:
Discipline cannot be outsourced. Your habits become your allies or jailers depending on your daily choices.

---

8 · Moderation Rule

युक्ताहारविहारस्य युक्तचेष्टस्य कर्मसु।

युक्तस्वप्नावबोधस्य योगो भवति दुःखहा॥ – **BG 6.17**

"For one balanced in food, recreation, effort, sleep, and wakefulness, Yoga destroys sorrow."

Applied today: regulate diet, rest, and digital intake. Balance isn't boredom—it's stamina's secret.

---

9 · The Lamp in Windless Place

यथा दीपो निवातस्थो नेङ्गते सोपमा स्मृता।

योगिनो यतचित्तस्य युञ्जतो योगमात्मनः॥ – **BG 6.19**

"As a lamp in a windless place does not flicker, so is the mind of a yogi in meditation."

Commentary:
Focus is inner still air. Create environments—quiet mornings, clean desks—that shelter your inner flame.

---

10 · Habit as Offering

तस्मादसक्तः सततं कार्यं कर्म समाचर।

असक्तो ह्याचरन् कर्म परमाप्नोति पुरुषः॥ – **BG 3.19**

"Therefore, unattached, perform duty constantly; performing without attachment, man attains the supreme."

Commentary:

Consistency (*satataṁ*) is explicitly prescribed. Daily, not dramatic, effort leads to liberation.

---

11 · When Laziness Masquerades as Peace

नियतं कुरु कर्म त्वं कर्म ज्यायो ह्यकर्मणः॥ – **BG 3.8**

"Perform your bounden duty; action is better than inaction."

Modern distortion equates spirituality with avoidance. The Gītā flips that: peace is born from participation without possessiveness.

---

12 · The Three Gunās of Consistency

रजो रागात्मकं वद्धि तृष्णासङ्गसमुद्भवम्।

तमस्त्वज्ञानजं वद्धि मोहनं सर्वदेहिनाम्॥ – BG 14.7-8

"Rajas springs from craving and attachment; Tamas from ignorance and inertia."

Commentary:

Every day you oscillate:

- **Tamas** – scrolling, delay, dullness
- **Rajas** – overdrive, restlessness
- **Sattva** – clarity, rhythm

  Discipline = increasing Sattva moments through mindful design.

---

13 · Faith in Process

श्रद्धावान् लभते ज्ञानं तत्परः संयतेन्द्रियः॥ – BG 4.39

"The faithful, self-controlled, devoted one attains knowledge."

Faith (*śraddhā*) here means steady trust in repetition. Keep practising meditation, study, exercise—even when nothing seems to happen. Results ripen invisibly.

14 · Grace of Perseverance

नहि कल्याणकृत्कश्चिद्दुर्गति तित गच्छति॥ – **BG 6.40**

"One who strives for good never meets ruin."

Every sincere effort is recorded in the universe's memory. Missed one day? Resume—the account retains credit.

15 · Ultimate Freedom Through Discipline

योगिनामपि सर्वेषां मद्गतेनान्तरा त्मना।

श्रद्धावान्भजते यो मां स मे युक्ततमो मतः॥ – **BG 6.47**

"Of all yogis, he who worships Me with steadfast faith, his inner self absorbed in Me, is deemed most united."

Commentary:
Union (*yoga*) is consistency of remembrance. The mature seeker turns every action into quiet devotion—writing code, cooking, teaching, parenting. Nothing is outside practice.

16 · Applied Modern Approach — Consistency Blueprint

Ancient Principle	Modern Practice	Outcome
Tapas – Discipline born of purpose	Fixed morning start; phone-free first hour	Mental order
Nishkāma karma – Work without clinging	Focus on effort metrics, not likes/sales	Reduced anxiety
Samatva – Equanimity	Journal one gratitude + one lesson daily	Emotional balance
Yuktāhāra – Moderation	Scheduled meals/sleep, digital diet	Physical steadiness
Śraddhā – Faithful repetition	Commit 40 days to one small vow	Habit consolidation

Add a simple ritual around each: lighting a lamp before work, one silent breath before replying to messages, or ending the day with a short verse. The body learns rhythm; the mind follows.

---

17 · Story Bridge — Arun Revisited

Three months later, Arun's mornings looked different:
– Wake → Water → Meditate 10 min → Write three lines of gratitude → Then phone.
He noticed something subtle: work felt lighter, not because

tasks reduced, but because resistance had.

The outer battlefield hadn't changed—email floods, deadlines, family expectations—but the inner soldier had learned formation.

---

18 · The Daily Mantra

नयितं कुरु कर्म त्वं तस्मादसक्तः सततं।

"Perform your duty regularly and without attachment."

Print one verse that resonates and keep it visible; repetition anchors will.

Consistency doesn't demand superhuman effort—just sacred regularity.

---

19 · Closing Reflection

Discipline is love expressed through time.

Every repetition declares: *I value this enough to return tomorrow.*

The *Bhagavad Gītā* maps that devotion into life's chaos—equanimity amid success, steadiness amid scrolls, silence amid schedules.

The secret isn't to fight distraction but to feed order until it hums louder.

सत्येनोत्तभिता भूमिः सूर्येण तपसा धृतः। – **Atharva Veda 12.1.1**

"The earth stands by truth; the sun by steadfast discipline."

Let your life, like the sun, rise every day to its dharma—quietly, reliably, unshakably.

Chapter 5

The Mirror Within: Knowing Your True Self

(Part 1 – The Search)

1 · The Many Masks

Mira was successful on paper—strategy head of a start-up, popular on social media, loved at home.Yet some mornings she woke heavy, as though each role she played—employee, partner, influencer—pulled her in a different direction.In meetings she was sharp; at night she scrolled endlessly through curated perfection, wondering who she really was behind all those tabs.

Burnout is rarely about doing too much; it is about forgetting who does it.

The Upaniṣads call this forgetfulness *Avidyā*—ignorance of one's own Self.

---

2 · The Ancient Mirror

असतो मा सद्गमय।

तमसो मा ज्योतिर्गमय।

मृत्योर्माऽमृतं गमय॥

asato mā sad gamaya |

tamaso mā jyotir gamaya |

mṛtyor mā 'mṛtaṁ gamaya ||

(Bṛhadāraṇyaka Upaniṣad 1.3.28)

Translation:
"Lead me from the unreal to the real, from darkness to light, from death to immortality."

Commentary:
Every digital refresh is a small prayer for this movement—from the unreal images of ourselves toward the enduring witness within.
Consistency begins when we act from the *real*, not from borrowed identities.

---

3 · The Hidden Self

नायमात्मा प्रवचनेन लभ्यो

न मेधया न बहुना श्रुतेन।

यमेवैष वृणुते तेन लभ्यः।

nāyam ātmā pravacanena labhyo
na medhayā na bahunā śrutena |

yamevaiṣa vṛṇute tena labhyaḥ ||

(Kaṭha Upaniṣad 1.2.23)

Translation:
"The Self is not attained by much learning or eloquence; it reveals itself to the one it chooses—one who longs sincerely."

Commentary:
Information isn't transformation. Self-knowledge arrives not through scrolling insights but through still sincerity.
Mira's mind consumed data; her heart needed devotion.

---

4 · The Flame That Watches

न तत्र सूर्यो भाति न चन्द्रतारकं

नेमा विद्युतो भान्ति कुतोऽयमग्निः।

तमेव भान्तमनुभाति सर्वं

तस्य भासा सर्वमिदं विभाति॥

na tatra sūryo bhāti na candra-tārakaṁ |

nemā vidyuto bhānti kuto'yam agniḥ |

tameva bhāntam anubhāti sarvaṁ |

tasya bhāsā sarvam idaṁ vibhāti ||

(Kaṭha Upaniṣad 2.2.15)

Translation:
"There the sun shines not, nor the moon nor stars;
by Its light all these shine."

Commentary:
Awareness itself is that light. Each time you observe your own thoughts without judging, you glimpse this *Ātman*—the silent witness that never flickers.

Modern practice: spend two minutes daily watching the breath as if watching a sunrise behind the mind.

---

5 · The River and the Sea

यथा नद्यः स्यन्दमानाः समुद्रेऽस्तं गच्छन्ति नामरूपे विहाय।

तथा विद्वान् नामरूपाद्विमुक्तः परात्परं पुरुषमुपैति दिव्यम्॥

yathā nadyaḥ syandamānāḥ samudre'staṁ gacchanti nāma-rūpe vihāya |

tathā vidvān nāma-rūpād vimuktaḥ parāt-paraṁ puruṣam

upaiti divyam ||

(Muṇḍaka Upaniṣad 3.2.8)

Translation:

"As rivers flowing enter the ocean, losing name and form, so the wise, freed from name and form, merge into the Supreme."

Commentary:

Identity-anxiety fades when one realises individuality is expression, not essence.

Work roles, relationship labels, online avatars—rivers; the Self—ocean.

Applied insight: act fully in each role, but return nightly to stillness, remembering *I am more than my functions.*

---

6 · The Knower and the Known

द्वा सुपर्णा सयुजा सखाया

समानं वृक्षं परिषस्वजाते।

तयोरन्यः पिप्पलं स्वाद्वत्त्यनश्नन्नन्यो अभिचाकशीति॥

dvā suparṇā sayujā sakhāyā

samānaṁ vṛkṣaṁ pariṣasvajāte |

tayor anyaḥ pippalaṁ svādv att yanaśnan anyo abhicākaśīti ||

(Muṇḍaka Upaniṣad 3.1.1)

Translation:
"Two birds, inseparable friends, perch on the same tree.
One eats the sweet fruit; the other simply watches."

Commentary:
The first bird is personality tasting experiences; the second is the witnessing Self.
Mindfulness revives that silent bird within—seeing without clinging.

---

7 . The One Behind Many

सर्वं खल्वदिं ब्रह्म।

sarvaṁ khalv idaṁ brahma

(Chāndogya Upaniṣad 3.14.1)

Translation:
"All this indeed is Brahman."

Commentary:

When awareness is steady, division dissolves.

Emails, conversations, chores—each shimmer with the same consciousness.

Consistency thus becomes reverence: doing the small as if serving the whole.

---

8 · Thou Art That

तत्त्वमसि श्वेतकेतो।

tat tvam asi śvetaketo

(Chāndogya Upaniṣad 6.8.7)

Translation:

"Thou art That, Śvetaketu."

Commentary:

The most famous equation of Vedānta equates the individual and the Absolute.

Remembering this during chaos re-centres the mind instantly.

In corporate stress or relational friction, silently repeat: *Tat Tvam Asi*—I am not this agitation; I am the awareness behind it.

Ancient Insight	Modern Parallel	Consistency Habit
Śravaṇa – listening to truth	Read/watch one page of timeless wisdom daily	Nourishes higher perspective
Manana – reflecting deeply	Journal 5 minutes on “Who was I before today’s roles?”	Restores self-awareness
Nididhyāsana – meditative absorption	10 minutes silent sitting	Stabilises identity beyond noise

9 · Modern Integration So Far

The Upaniṣads outline three consistent practices for modern seekers:

Through these micro-rituals, Mira began shifting.
Instead of identifying as "burned-out strategist," she started seeing herself as awareness expressing through that strategist.
Her schedule didn't shrink—but her suffering did.

Chapter 5

The Mirror Within: Knowing Your True Self

(Part 2 – Living from Awareness)

---

1 · The Modern Noise

Even after Mira's initial awakening, distraction stalked her.
Deadlines demanded speed; social feeds demanded presence; relationships demanded empathy.
How could she stay inwardly anchored while still engaged in a fast-moving world?

The Gītā answers: by acting **through** awareness, not **for** identity.

---

2 · The Witness in Action

प्रकाशं च प्रवृत्तिं च मोहमेव च पाण्डव।

न द्वेष्टि संप्रवृत्तानि न निवृत्तानि काङ्क्षति॥

prakāśaṁ ca pravṛttiṁ ca moham eva ca pāṇḍava

na dveṣṭi saṁpravṛttāni na nivṛttāni kāṅkṣati – BG 14.22

Translation:
"When light, action, or delusion arise, he neither hates them nor longs for their absence."

Commentary:
Consistency of self-awareness means observing changing moods like passing clouds.
Instead of "I am angry," see "Anger is passing through me."
This is the start of unshakeable emotional intelligence.

---

3 · The Yogi's Steadiness

सुखदुःखे समे कृत्वा लाभालाभौ जयाजयौ।

ततो युद्धाय युज्यस्व नैवं पापमवाप्स्यसि॥

sukha-duḥkhe same kṛtvā lābhālābhau jayājayau

tato yuddhāya yujyasva naivaṁ pāpam avāpsyasi – BG 2.38

Translation:
"Equating pleasure and pain, gain and loss, victory and defeat—engage in your duty; such equanimity frees you from fault."

Commentary:
In careers and relationships, inner steadiness is moral cleanliness.
When outcomes no longer define worth, action regains purity.

---

4 · The Controlled Mind

यतो यतो निश्चरति मनश्चञ्चलमस्थिरम्।

ततस्ततो नियम्यैतदात्मन्येव वशं नयेत्॥

yato yato niścarati manaś cañcalam asthiram

tatas tato niyamya itad ātmany eva vaśaṁ nayet – BG 6.26

Translation:
"Wherever the restless mind wanders, let him gently bring it back under the control of the Self."

Commentary:
This verse is mindfulness distilled: consistency is not about never wandering, but about always returning.
Every recall strengthens awareness muscles.

---

5 · Stillness as Strength

योगश्चित्तवृत्तिनिरोधः॥

yogaś citta-vṛtti-nirodhaḥ – Yoga Sūtra 1.2

Translation:
"Yoga is the stilling of the fluctuations of the mind."

Commentary:
The battlefield is inside.
When thought-waves quiet, one meets the mirror-lake Self.

Begin with 5 minutes daily of attention to breath—nothing fancy, just faithful repetition.

---

6 · The Observer Beyond Roles

द्रष्टा दृशिमात्रः शुद्धोऽपि प्रत्ययानुपश्यः॥

draṣṭā dṛśi-mātraḥ śuddho'pi pratyayānupaśyaḥ – Yoga Sūtra 2.20

Translation:
"The Seer is pure seeing, though witnessing thoughts as they arise."

Commentary:
Behind profession, gender, opinions, there is pure seeing—constant, unstained.
Whenever you feel fragmented, pause and ask: *Who is noticing this?*
That question reboots identity to its default clarity.

---

7 · Inner Contentment

संतोषात् अनुत्तमः सुखलाभः॥

santoṣāt anuttamaḥ sukha-lābhaḥ – Yoga Sūtra 2.42

Translation:

"From contentment comes supreme happiness."

Commentary:

Contentment (*santoṣa*) is the emotional form of consistency—being equally at ease with what is.

Gratitude journals, mindful meals, screen-free evenings: simple acts that train the nervous system to stay calm rather than crave more.

---

8 · The Self Shining Alone

एको देवः सर्वभूतेषु गूढः सर्वव्यापी सर्वभूतान्तरात्मा।

eko devaḥ sarva-bhūteṣu gūḍhaḥ sarva-vyāpī sarva-bhūtāntar-ātmā – Śvetāśvatara Upaniṣad 6.11

Translation:

"One divine Self hidden in all beings, all-pervading, the inner soul of all."

Commentary:

Knowing this removes loneliness.
Whether in a meeting, relationship, or scrolling feed—you are never outside divinity; you're simply distracted from it.

---

9 · Applied Modern Synthesis: The Practice of Inner Consistency

The scriptures outline a shift from **identification** to **observation**, from **reaction** to **response**.
Modern life offers endless triggers; self-knowledge converts them into training grounds.

The Self-Reflection Algorithm

1. **Pause → Pratyāhāra (Withdrawal):**
   Before reacting to stimuli (email, argument, craving), take one conscious breath.
   This interrupts mechanical identity and returns you to awareness.
2. **Observe → Draṣṭā-bhāva (Witness mode):**

   Ask: *Who is aware of this thought?*

Recognise that the witness is unchanged whether praised or blamed.

3. **Discern → Viveka (Clarity):**
   Identify which impulse arises from fleeting emotion and which from values.
   Follow the latter.
4. **Align → Karma-Yoga:**
   Act decisively but offer the result back to the whole—
   īśvara-arpaṇa-buddhi.

   Work becomes meditation.
5. **Anchor → Nididhyāsana (Contemplation):**
   End each day with two minutes of inner check-in: *Was I aware, or merely busy?*
   Note without judgment; restart tomorrow.

This five-step loop practised daily re-programs the mind for steadiness.

---

10 · Mira's Integration

Three months later, Mira's calendar remained full, but her centre stopped spinning.
In the office, she scheduled silent two-minute pauses before major calls.
In relationships, she replaced defensive words with one breath.

Online, she practised *digital santoṣa*—closing the feed when envy stirred.

Friends called her calmer; she called it *coming home.*

---

11 · Daily Anchors

Practice	Verse Reminder	Real-World Expression
Morning stillness	***"Yogaś citta-vṛtti-nirodhaḥ"***	**5 min mindful breathing**
Mid-day equanimity	***"Sukha-duḥkhe same kṛtvā…"***	**Respond, don't react**
Evening gratitude	***"Santoṣāt anuttamaḥ sukha-lābhaḥ"***	**Write 3 things done well**

Small repetitions, big rewiring. The Self does not grow; the noise just subsides.

---

12 · Closing Reflection

नायमात्मा बलहीनेन लभ्यः।

nāyam ātmā balahīnena labhyaḥ – Muṇḍaka Upaniṣad 3.2.4

"The Self is not attained by the weak."
Strength here means steadiness—the quiet power of showing up for yourself daily.

Self-knowledge isn't mystical escapism; it's the most practical consistency skill on earth.
When you act from awareness rather than identity, burnout turns to flow, comparison to inspiration, and relationships to mirrors of growth.

तत्त्वमसि – You are That.

Remember, repeat, realise.

---

13 · Chapter Summary

- **Core Idea:** Knowing the Self dissolves inner contradiction—the root of inconsistency.
- **Key Scriptures:** Upaniṣads, Bhagavad Gītā 6, 14, 2; Yoga Sūtras 1–2.

- **Daily Algorithm:** Pause → Observe → Discern → Align → Anchor.
- **Outcome:** Unbroken awareness amid modern complexity—true *Unshakable* living.

Chapter 6

The Cycle Trap: Escaping Modern Saṁsāra

---

1 · The Endless Scroll

Dev had it all — a fast career, an on-and-off relationship, and a phone that never slept.
He checked messages while brushing, emails during meals, reels before bed.

Weekends were "self-care," which meant more scrolling in softer light.
Every Monday felt like rebirth, every Friday like death — a small Saṁsāra repeating weekly.

The ancients named this *bhava-cakra*, the wheel of becoming: craving → striving → fatigue → craving again.
Modern life simply digitised it.

---

2 · The Law of Repetition

यथा कर्म यथा श्रुतम्।

yathā karma yathā śrutam – Bṛhadāraṇyaka Upaniṣad 4.4.6

Translation:
"As one acts and as one thinks, so one becomes."

Commentary:
The mind doesn't forget patterns; it automates them.
Every scroll, every stress-response, every emotional outburst writes another karmic line of code.
Consistency can enslave or liberate depending on what we repeat.

---

3 · The Snare of Desire

ध्यायतो वषियान्पुंसः सङ्गस्तेषूपजायते।

सङ्गात् संजायते कामः कामात् क्रोधोऽभजिायते॥

dhyāyato viṣayān puṁsaḥ saṅgas teṣū pajāyate |

saṅgāt sañjāyate kāmaḥ kāmāt krodho'bhijāyate || – BG 2.62

Translation:
"Dwelling on sense objects brings attachment; from attachment arises desire; from desire, anger."

Commentary:
Every notification is bait. The loop begins with attention. Freedom starts by reclaiming what we *choose* to contemplate.

---

4 · The Mind's Machinery

असंशयं महाबाहो मनो दुर्नग्रिहं चलम्।

अभ्यासेन तु कौन्तेय वैराग्येण च गृह्यते॥

asaṁśayaṁ mahā-bāho mano durnigrahaṁ calam |

abhyāsena tu kaunteya vairāgyeṇa ca gṛhyate || – BG 6.35

Translation:

"The mind is restless and hard to control, but by practice and detachment it is mastered."

Commentary:

Algorithms feed distraction; only *abhyāsa* (steady practice) rewrites them.

Each time Dev paused before checking his phone, he weakened the loop a little.

---

5 · The Mirage of Achievement

न हि तृप्तिं लभते कामैः पुनः पुनर्विवर्धितैः।

na hi tṛptiṁ labhate kāmaiḥ punaḥ punar vivardhitaiḥ –

Manusmṛti 2.94

Translation:

"Desires multiplied again and again never bring satisfaction."

Commentary:

Promotion, purchase, post — each gives a flicker, then hunger returns.

The consumer cycle is the modern *saṁsāra-cakra* spinning faster.

6 · The Burnout Loop

त्रैगुण्यविषया वेदा निस्त्रैगुण्यो भवार्जुन।

traiguṇya-viṣayā vedā nistrai-guṇyo bhavārjuna – BG 2.45

Translation:

"The world of the three guṇas is flux; rise beyond them, O Arjuna."

Commentary:

Rajas drives ambition, Tamas fuels exhaustion, Sattva brings clarity.

Consistency means learning to surf these waves rather than drown in them.

---

7 · The Mirror of Relationship

न द्वेष्टि सम्प्रवृत्तानि न निवृत्तानि काङ्क्षति॥

na dveṣṭi sampravṛttāni na nivṛttāni kāṅkṣati – BG 14.22

Translation:

"He neither hates when emotions arise nor longs when they fade."

Commentary:

Love's loop — desire → attachment → fear of loss — ends only through witnessing affection without ownership.
Dev's repeated heartbreak softened when he stopped needing control.

---

8 · The Wheel of Habit

यदा भूतपृथग्भावमेकस्थमनुपश्यति।

ततः एव च विस्तारं ब्रह्म सम्पद्यते तदा॥

yadā bhūta-pṛthag-bhāvam eka-stham anupaśyati |

tata eva ca vistāraṁ brahma sampadyate tadā – BG 13.30

Translation:

"When one sees all diverse actions resting in One, he attains Brahman."

Commentary:

Recognising the sameness of cycles—work stress, digital

craving, relationship drama—helps transcend them. Awareness, not escape, ends repetition.

---

9 · The Restless River

चलप्रकृतिस्त्वं स्थिरोऽसि चेतसा।

cala-prakṛtis tvaṁ sthiro'si cetasā – Mahābhārata Śānti Parva 321.10

Translation:
"Though nature is moving, be steady in consciousness."

Commentary:
External motion is inevitable; inner steadiness is optional. The wise don't fight change; they stand still at the centre.

---

10 · The Observer's Seat

द्रष्टा दृशिमात्रः शुद्धोऽपि प्रत्ययानुपश्यः॥

draṣṭā dṛśi-mātraḥ śuddho'pi pratyayānupaśyaḥ – Yoga Sūtra 2.20

Translation:

"The Seer is pure awareness, witnessing thought patterns."

Commentary:

Stepping back from the mind's movie breaks identification. Once you see the reel, you are no longer trapped in the plot.

---

11 · The Breath Break

प्राणापानौ समौ कृत्वा नासाभ्यन्तरचारिणौ।

prāṇāpānau samau kṛtvā nāsābhyantara-cāriṇau – BG 5.27

Translation:

"Balancing inhalation and exhalation, controlling the movements of breath."

Commentary:

Conscious breathing is the oldest de-bugger of Saṁsāra.

Every slow exhale resets neural rhythm and re-aligns attention with awareness.

---

12 · The Moment of Insight

यदा विनियतं चित्तमात्मन्येवावतिष्ठते।

निःस्पृहः सर्वकामेभ्यो युक्त इत्युच्यते तदा॥

yadā viniyataṁ cittam ātmany evāvatishṭhate |

niḥspṛhaḥ sarva-kāmebhyo yukta ity ucyate tadā – BG 6.18

Translation:
"When the controlled mind rests in the Self, free from craving, that is true Yoga."

Commentary:
The finish line isn't absence of work, phones, or love—it's presence without dependence.

---

13 · The Breaking of the Wheel

भवबन्धविमोक्षोऽस्य ज्ञानमेव न संशयः।

bhava-bandha-vimokṣo 'sya jñānam eva na saṁśayaḥ –

Viveka-Cūḍāmaṇi 56

Translation:

"Knowledge alone breaks the bondage of becoming—no doubt."

Commentary:

Seeing the loop clearly is 80 % of freedom.
The rest is gentle discipline—walking differently after noticing the circle.

---

14 · The Quiet Mind

नवृित्तरिूपं च सुखं लभन्ते।

nivṛtti-rūpaṁ ca sukhaṁ labhante – Taittirīya Upaniṣad 2.7.1

Translation:

"They attain happiness whose joy is of stillness."

Commentary:

True pleasure isn't stimulation but cessation — the peace after the refresh button stops clicking.

---

15 · Liberation Algorithm – How to Step Off the Wheel

Step	Sanskrit Cue	Practical Application
1. Awareness (Smṛti)	*dhyāyato viṣayān puṁsaḥ...*	Notice triggers — the first scroll, the first craving, the first irritation.
2. Interruption (Pratyāhāra)	*abhyāsena tu kaunteya...*	Replace impulse with breath; delay by 10 seconds.
3. Re-alignment (Viveka)	*yathā karma yathā śrutam*	Ask: "Will this act expand or shrink my awareness?"
4. Action (Karma-Yoga)	*tasmād asaktaḥ satataṁ kāryaṁ karma samācara*	Do the necessary task, detached from praise.
5. Rest (Nididhyāsana)	*nivṛtti-rūpaṁ ca sukhaṁ labhante*	End each day with 5 minutes of silence; let the

		wheel stop spinning.

Repeated daily, this algorithm converts loops into spirals—each turn rising a little higher instead of circling flat.

---

16 · Dev's Awakening

A year later, Dev's schedule remained full: meetings, relationships, messages.
But something had changed—he paused before reacting, breathed before replying, and logged off without FOMO.
He still moved through cycles, but the cycles no longer moved through him.

He realised Saṁsāra is not a place we escape; it's a pattern we outgrow.

---

17 · Closing Reflection

मृत्युः स मृत्युं आप्नोति य इह नानेव पश्यति।

mṛtyuḥ sa mṛtyuṁ āpnoti ya iha nāneva paśyati – Kaṭha Upaniṣad 2.1.11

Translation:
"He goes from death to death who sees difference as real."

Commentary:
Fragmentation—between work and rest, online and offline, self and others—keeps the wheel spinning.
Wholeness ends repetition.

The goal isn't to run away from Saṁsāra but to see through it—to live in rhythm, not in reaction.
Then every scroll, task, and touch becomes sacred, not cyclic.

"The wheel turns, but the centre is still."

Live from that centre.
That is liberation-in-motion.
That is the consistency of freedom—**the Unshakable state.**

Chapter 7

The Law of Invisible Effort: Karma Yoga in the Age of Noise

1 · A young professional—Ananya—feels invisible at work. She delivers projects, yet recognition goes to louder colleagues. Online she sees "overnight" successes and begins to doubt quiet effort.

One evening she reads: *"The Sun never announces its dawn."*

This becomes the thread of the chapter: **how unseen, consistent work creates real transformation**.

---

2 · Scriptural framework (15 śloka set)

#	Source	Key idea	Modern-age problem it answers
1	**Bhagavad Gītā 2.47** *karmaṇy evādhikāras te…*	Right to action, not results	Anxiety over outcomes, performance reviews
2	**Gītā 3.19** *tasmād asaktaḥ satataṁ kāryaṁ karma samācara*	Duty without attachment	Burnout from constant comparison
3	**Gītā 12.16** *anapekṣaḥ śuciḥ*	Purity & detachment	Social-media validation addiction

	dakṣa udāsīno gata-vyathaḥ		
4	**Gītā 4.41** *yoga-saṁnyasta-karmāṇam jñāna-saṁchinna-saṁśayam*	Knowledge dissolves doubt	Decision paralysis
5	**Gītā 18.66** *sarva-dharmān parityajya mām ekaṁ śaraṇaṁ vraja*	Surrender to higher order	Loss of control / uncertainty
6	**Kaṭha Upaniṣad 2.3.14** *uttishthata jāgrata…*	Arise and awaken	Chronic procrastination
7	**Muṇḍaka Upaniṣad 1.2.13** *yasya śraddhā satya-bhāvā…*	Faith strengthens effort	Self-doubt, imposter syndrome
8	**Taittirīya Upaniṣad 1.11.2** *satyaṁ vada, dharmaṁ cara*	Integrity in action	Ethical compromise at work
9	**Yoga Sūtra 2.1** *tapaḥ svādhyāya īśvara-*	Three-fold path of discipline	Distraction, lack of focus

	praṇidhānāni kriyā-yogaḥ		
10	**Yoga Sūtra 2.47** *prayatna-śaithilya-ananta-samāpatti-bhyaṁ*	Effortless effort	Stress and perfectionism
11	**Mahābhārata Śānti Parva 12.290.7** *na hi kāryaṁ vinā karma...*	Work is unavoidable	Escapism / spiritual bypassing
12	**Bhāgavata Purāṇa 11.19.36** *kṛtajño dāntaḥ śāntaḥ...*	Gratitude & restraint	Entitlement culture
13	**Gītā 3.30** *mayi sarvāṇi karmāṇi sannyasya adhyātma-cetasaḥ*	Offering work to the Divine	Ego fatigue in leadership
14	**Gītā 12.12** *śreyo hi jñānam abhyāsāj jñānād dhyānam viśiṣyate*	Practice > theory > contemplation	Information overload
15	**Bhagavad Gītā 6.40** *na hi kalyaṇa-kṛt*	No good effort is wasted	Fear of failure

kaścit du र्गतिं *tāta*

gacchati

---

3 · Integrating verse + commentary (sample paragraphs)

Verse 1 – Gītā 2.47

"Your right is to action alone…"
Consistency in unseen labour is sanity's safeguard. The verse unhooks effort from applause.
Solution: measure progress by integrity of input, not external metrics. Replace daily performance tracking with "Did I give my best attention today?"

Verse 3 – Gītā 12.16

"He who is unexpectant, pure, efficient, detached…"
Modern translation: Be professional, not performative.
Solution: digital fasts, muted notifications, weekly social-media sabbath.

Verse 9 – Yoga Sūtra 2.1

"Discipline, self-study, surrender constitute Yoga in action."
Solution:

- Tapas → micro-routines (wake time, movement)
- Svādhyāya → reflective journaling
- Īśvara-praṇidhāna → letting go of results

Consistency then becomes a spiritual workout: will, wisdom, and worship moving together.

Verse 10 – Yoga Sūtra 2.47

"Perfection in posture is attained by relaxation of effort."
This paradox solves modern stress: loosen the ego's grip, not the schedule.
Solution: Mindful breaks, slower breathing before deadlines, "soft focus" in meetings.

---

4 · Solutions map (scripture → modern problem)

Modern issue	Scriptural principle	Practical practice
Burnout	*tasmād asaktaḥ satataṁ kāryaṁ karma samācara*	Work in focused intervals, detach emotionally after each task.

Social comparison	*anapekṣaḥ śuciḥ dakṣaḥ*	Daily gratitude note; limit screen comparison.
Procrastination	*uttishthata jāgrata*	"5-minute rule": start → momentum builds.
Anxiety over outcomes	*karmaṇy evādhikāras te*	Define effort goals, not result goals.
Ethical conflict	*satyaṁ vada, dharmaṁ cara*	Speak truth kindly; choose transparency over speed.
Perfectionism	*prayatna-śaithilya*	Pause, exhale, resume—let excellence flow, not force.

---

5 · Narrative interludes (to weave between verses)

- **Work:** Ananya learns to schedule "invisible blocks" for quiet deep work, resisting instant praise culture.
- **Relationships:** Applying *santoṣa*, she practises gratitude instead of expectations, reducing resentment loops.

- **Digital life:** Each phone-unlock becomes a mindfulness bell; she silently repeats *mayi sarvāṇi karmāṇi sannyasya...* before posting.

---

6 · Practical daily routine ("Invisible Effort Algorithm")

1. **Intention (Ārambha):** Morning 3 breaths + recite *karmaṇy evādhikāras te.*
2. **Execution (Kriyā):** 90-minute distraction-free sprints.
3. **Reflection (Svādhyāya):** Note one lesson, not one metric.
4. **Offering (Ārpaṇa):** Close laptop → silently dedicate effort.
5. **Repose (Viśrānti):** Evening stillness; remember *na hi kalyaṇa-kṛt kaścit du रगति gacchati.*

---

7 · Closing reflection

Invisible effort is the quiet Dharma of our time. Algorithms may reward virality, but existence rewards sincerity.

Every disciplined act—an unposted kindness, an unseen hour of focus—adds weight to inner gravity.

"No good effort is ever lost." – BG 6.40

When actions become offerings, life regains rhythm: less oscillation, more flow.
In the still centre of consistent service, anxiety dissolves; the worker and the work merge.
That is the **Law of Invisible Effort**—modern Karma Yoga applied.
Act well, release, repeat.
Unshakable.

Chapter 8

The Liberation Code: Mokṣa in the Modern Mind

1 · **Arjun Mehta—CEO by** thirty-five, always on call, always adored.

Yet each quarterly win left a quieter ache.

His partner, Leela, felt unseen; his phone buzzed through dinners; sleep came only in fragments of blue light.

He owned everything except rest.

One evening, during a flight delay, he asked himself a question that changed him:

"If success is freedom, why do I feel caged?"

That night begins the journey from bondage through **Karma (action), Prema (love), and Jñāna (knowledge)** toward **Mokṣa — freedom in engagement**.

---

2 · Corporate Bondage → Karma to Karma-Yoga

Scripture	Verse	Key line	Modern insight

Bhagavad Gītā 2.47	*karmaṇy evādhikāras te mā phaleṣu kadācana*	"Your right is to action, not to its fruits."	Success anxiety ends when work becomes offering.
Gītā 5.12	*yuktah karma-phalaṁ tyaktvā śāntim āpnoti naiṣṭhikīm*	"The disciplined man, renouncing results, attains abiding peace."	Do the task, release the tension.
Gītā 18.66	*sarva-dharmān parityajya mām ekaṁ śaraṇaṁ vraja*	"Abandon all duties to Me alone surrender."	Let go of control → gain creative flow.
Taittirīya Upaniṣad 1.11.2	*satyaṁ vada dharmaṁ cara*	"Speak truth; act by righteousness."	Integrity as productivity—peace replaces pressure.

Yoga Sūtra 2.47	*prayatna-śaithilya-ananta-samāpatti-bhyām*	"Perfection comes by relaxing effort and merging into the infinite."	Sustainable excellence = effort − ego.

Mini-commentary:

Arjun reframed meetings as meditations: *do, deliver, detach.*

Productivity rose; panic fell.

The board called it efficiency; he called it surrender.

---

3 · Relationship Bondage → Love without Possession

Scripture	Verse	Key line	Modern insight
Bhagavad Gītā 12.13–14	*adveṣṭā sarva-bhūtānāṁ maitraḥ karuṇa eva ca*	"Free from hatred, friendly, compassionate."	Love = empathy without ownership.

Rāmāyaṇa Ayodhyā Kāṇḍa 1.18	*rāmo vigrahavān dharmaḥ*	"Rāma is righteousness embodied."	Duty sustains affection; promises protect trust.
Gītā 6.32	*ātmaupamyena sarvatra samaṁ paśyati yo arjuna*	"He who sees all beings as himself..."	Emotional maturity = perspective parity.
Kaṭha Upaniṣad 2.3.14	*uttishthata jāgrata prāpya varān nibodhata*	"Arise, awake, learn from the wise."	Self-work before love-work.
Bhāgavata Purāṇa 11.19.33	*ātmaupamyena sarveṣām dayā kāryā yathātmani*	"Show the same compassion to all as to yourself."	Healthy boundaries born of reverence.

Mini-commentary:

Leela once needed constant reassurance; Arjun needed admiration.

Through daily *metta-style* reflection on "May all be happy," both learned that affection expands when ownership ends. Their bond matured from demand to devotion.

4 · Digital Bondage → Silence as Luxury

Scripture	Verse	Key line	Modern insight
Kaṭha Upaniṣad 2.1.10	*paraṁ guhyaṁ śrāvayed yo anubhūya*	"The supreme secret is realised, not advertised."	Depth over display; share less, sense more.
Gītā 6.26	*yato yato niścarati manaś cañcalam asthiram…*	"Wherever the mind wanders, bring it back."	Mindfulness over mind-traffic.
Yoga Sūtra 1.2	*yogaś citta-vṛtti-nirodhaḥ*	"Yoga is the stilling of thought-waves."	Digital detox = cognitive Yoga.
Śvetāśvatara Upaniṣad 6.15	*sarvaṁ karmāṇi manasā sannyasya*	"Renouncing mental action, he rests in peace."	Switch off to tune in.

	āste śāntam ātmānam		
Mahābhārata Śānti Parva 329.4	*maunaṁ hi paramaṁ tapaḥ*	"Silence is the highest austerity."	Logging out is new tapas.

Mini-commentary:

Arjun began one "silent hour" daily—no phone, no playlist, just breathing.

The mind initially screamed; later it sang.

From that quiet, creativity returned—proof that silence multiplies soundness.

---

5 · Synthesis — Three Chains, One Key

All forms of bondage share the same structure:

Attachment → Anxiety → Exhaustion.

The key in every scripture is the same word: *Tyāga — release.*

Gītā 5.10:

brahmaṇy ādhāya karmāṇi saṅgaṁ tyaktvā karoti yaḥ

"He who acts surrendering all to Brahman, free from attachment, is untouched by sin—like a lotus by water."

Modern translation: work, love, and connect—but stay afloat.

---

6 · Practical Solutions — "Mokṣa Algorithm"

Step	Scriptural cue	Daily application
1. Observe bondage	*dhyāyato viṣayān puṁsaḥ* (BG 2.62)	Notice cravings for praise, control, attention.
2. Pause & breathe	*yato yato niścarati manaḥ* (BG 6.26)	Three conscious breaths before reacting.
3. Re-frame action	*karmaṇy evādhikāras te* (BG 2.47)	Focus on input quality, not output image.
4. Offer up results	*mayi sarvāṇi karmāṇi sannyasya* (BG 3.30)	Mentally dedicate work to higher purpose.
5. Withdraw daily	*maunaṁ hi paramaṁ tapaḥ*	30-min digital silence.
6. Serve others	*ātmaupamyena sarvatra samaṁ paśyati*	Compassion projects or mentorship.

7. Contemplate unity	*sarvaṁ khalv idaṁ brahma*	Remind yourself: everything you touch is divine matter.

7 · Arjun's Liberation

Six months later, quarterly profits still rose—but he no longer chased them.

He delegated more, listened longer, and spent evenings in quiet dinners without devices.

He and Leela walked each night, discussing gratitude instead of grievances.

One weekend, he left his phone at home entirely; Monday's anxiety never came back.

Freedom hadn't meant quitting work, love, or technology—it meant quitting *dependence*.

He realised Mokṣa is not withdrawal from the world but awakening *within* it.

8 · Closing Reflection

Bṛhadāraṇyaka Upaniṣad 4.4.14:

sa ya ātmā tat tvam asi – "That Self—thou art."

Gītā 6.27:

prapaśyanti munayaḥ śāntaṁ brahma nairguṇyam avyayam –

"The serene see the eternal, stainless Brahman."

Liberation is not a destination; it's a *consistent recognition*:
"I am not the role; I am the awareness playing it."
When that insight stabilises through daily practice, the corporate ladder, emotional waves, and digital noise lose power.
Action continues; agitation stops.
This is Mokṣa for the modern mind—**freedom in participation**.

---

9 · Key take-aways

- **Corporate fix:** Practice *Karma-Yoga*—perform, detach, rest.

- **Relationship fix:** Cultivate *Bhakti without Bhaṅga*—love without demand.
- **Digital fix:** Observe *Mauna and Pratyāhāra*—periodic silence, mindful media use.
- **Universal fix:** Remember *Tat Tvam Asi*—awareness is already free.

---

10 · End verse

Muṇḍaka Upaniṣad 3.2.9:

bhidyate hṛdaya-granthiś chidyante sarva-saṁśayāḥ,

kṣīyante cāsya karmāṇi tasmin dṛṣṭe parāvare

"When the Supreme is realised, the knots of the heart are cut, all doubts vanish, and all karma dissolves."

That is the Liberation Code—
not escape from effort, but release within effort.
Not renunciation of life, but reunion with its essence.
The still point in motion: **Unshakable Freedom.**

Chapter 9

The Inner Republic: Rebuilding Order in a Disordered Age

1·The Collapse Within

Cities shimmer at night like electric constellations—progress shining on the surface, but underneath, hearts burn with fatigue. People speak faster, sleep less, and trust sparingly. Governments promise transparency yet leak corruption; families live under one roof yet in separate worlds; the earth groans beneath human convenience.

Disorder isn't only in institutions—it begins in intention.

When the inner Dharma collapses, the outer republic follows.

This chapter seeks to rebuild from the inside out: *self-order → social order → ecological order.*

---

2 · The Seed of All Crisis

यदा यदा हि धर्मस्य ग्लानिर्भवति भारत।

अभ्युत्थानम् अधर्मस्य तदात्मानं सृजाम्यहम्॥

yadā yadā hi dharmasya glānir bhavati bhārata |
abhyutthānam adharmasya tadātmānaṁ sṛjāmy aham || –
Bhagavad Gītā 4.7

Translation:
"Whenever righteousness declines and unrighteousness rises, I manifest Myself."

Commentary:
Dharma doesn't only decay in history; it declines in each moment of apathy.
Corruption, exploitation, pollution—each begins with the small permission we grant ourselves to ignore what's right.

Traditional Solution:
The Gītā's response is not escapism but *restoration through awareness*.
Every individual must become an *avatāra* in miniature—a self-born force of correction in daily life: returning borrowed books, keeping promises, refusing bribes, respecting nature.
Small restorations, multiplied, become revival.

---

3 · Leadership Crisis — The Forgotten Rajarṣi Ideal

राजा धर्मेण भूमिं पालयति तेन स धर्मराज इति कथ्यते।

rājā dharmeṇa bhūmiṁ pālayati tena sa dharma-rāja iti kathyate – Mahābhārata Śānti Parva 88.3

Translation:
"A king who governs through Dharma is rightly called a Dharmarāja."

Commentary:
Leadership once meant stewardship; today it often means marketing.

The traditional model of *Rājarṣi* (king-sage) teaches balance—authority anchored in humility.

Solution:
Ancient polity insisted that rulers undergo *brahmacharya* (discipline) and *svādhyāya* (study) before ruling.
Applied today: leaders must serve apprenticeships in ethics and public welfare, not just economics.
Transparency born of tapasya, not regulation, sustains trust.

---

4 · Inequality — The Lost Vision of Harmony

चातुर्वर्ण्यं मया सृष्टं गुणकर्मविभागशः।

cātur-varṇyaṁ mayā sṛṣṭaṁ guṇa-karma-vibhāgaśaḥ – Bhagavad Gītā 4.13

Translation:
"The fourfold order was created by Me according to qualities and action."

Commentary:

Varṇa was never meant as caste by birth but as harmony by disposition and function.
Modern inequality stems from forgetting that diversity of talent is meant for mutual service, not hierarchy.

Solution:

Return to the principle of *Guṇa-Karma-Samatā*—equality of dignity, diversity of work.
In workplaces, teach cooperative dharma: value contribution, not background.
In society, revive the spirit of *seva*—service as spiritual equality.

---

5 · Family Strain — The Withering of Gṛhastha Dharma

गृहेषु नित्यं भव शान्तचित्तः।

gṛheṣu nityaṁ bhava śānta-cittaḥ – Manusmṛti 4.12

Translation:
"Dwell in your home with a tranquil mind."

Commentary:
The home is society's first temple.
When relationships become transactional, the outer world echoes that chaos.

Traditional Solution:
Ancient households observed *Sandhyā-vandana*—morning and evening prayers as collective rhythm.

Modern equivalent: a digital sunset rule—devices aside after dusk; shared silence, shared meals.
Family cohesion begins in shared stillness, not shared screens.

---

6 · Loneliness and Consumerism — The Hunger that Consumes

नति्यतृप्तो नरिाश्रयः।

nitya-tṛpto nirāśrayaḥ – Bhagavad Gītā 4.20

Translation:
"He who is ever content, dependent on none, is truly free."

Commentary:
Consumer culture thrives on manufactured incompleteness. Traditional wisdom reminds us that joy is generated inward, not purchased outward.

Solution:

Adopt *Santoṣa* (contentment) as a modern vow—buy less, use longer, give more.
Replace shopping rituals with sharing rituals.
Gratitude is the ancient wealth that cancels craving.

---

7 · Identity Politics and Division — The Forgetting of Oneness

एकोऽहम् बहुस्याम्।

eko'ham bahu-syām – Chāndogya Upaniṣad 6.2.3

Translation:
"I am One; let Me become many."

Commentary:
Diversity was born from unity, not opposition.
Social disunity arises when identity replaces essence.

Traditional Solution:
Revive *Sama-darśana*—equal vision.
Teach comparative study of scriptures, cross-community festivals, interfaith service.
Unity through awareness, not uniformity through force.

---

8 · Ecological Neglect — Losing Rhythm with Ṛta

माता भूमिः पुत्रोऽहं पृथिव्याः।

mātā bhūmiḥ putro'haṁ pṛthivyāḥ – Atharva Veda 12.1.12

Translation:
"The Earth is my mother, and I am her son."

Commentary:
Vedic ecology viewed the planet as sacred kinship, not resource.
Climate change reflects inner imbalance: greed outweighing gratitude.

Solution:
Perform *Bhūmi Pūjā* in spirit—treat consumption as offering, not exploitation.
Plant trees as prayer, recycle as tapas, live simply as worship.
Restoring Ṛta (cosmic order) begins with rhythm—use, pause, renew.

---

9 · Waste Culture — The Discipline of Simplicity

अपरगि्रहस्थैर्ये जन्मकथंतासंबोधः।

aparigraha-sthairye janma-kathantā-sambodhaḥ – *Yoga Sūtra 2.39*

Translation:
"When one is firmly established in non-possession, he comprehends the meaning of existence."

Commentary:
Minimalism isn't aesthetic; it's metaphysical clarity.
When clutter drops, consciousness sharpens.

Traditional Solution:
Practise *Aparigraha*—limit possessions to what serves Dharma. Quarterly cleansing of unused items, mindful consumption, and conscious gifting restore sacred order to matter.

---

10 · Moral Exhaustion — The Need for Tapas (Inner Fire)

तपसा जायते तेजः।

tapasā jāyate tejaḥ – *Atharva Veda 11.5.18*

Translation:
"Through discipline arises radiance."

Commentary:
Modern activism burns out because it lacks inner fire.

Tapas is not mere effort—it's consecrated energy, will purified by purpose.

Solution:
Combine activism with contemplation: every reformer must be a meditator.
Start mornings with silence before strategy; let advocacy arise from clarity, not anger.
That transforms outrage into luminous influence.

11·The Inner Republic Model

Ancient India saw the cosmos as a well-governed state—**Ṛta** at the top (cosmic law), **Dharma** in the middle (human law), and **Karma** at the base (personal law).
When the three align, prosperity follows.

Disorder	*Traditional Counter-Principle*	*Modern Practice*
Corruption	Satya (truth)	Public transparency, personal honesty, vow of truthfulness
Inequality	Seva (service)	Volunteer work, mentorship, economic fairness

Family strain	Saṁyama (moderation)	Shared prayer, digital boundaries
Loneliness	Satsaṅga (holy company)	Conscious communities, reading circles
Ecological neglect	Yajña (sacrifice for collective good)	Sustainable living, carbon compassion
Waste culture	Aparigraha (non-hoarding)	Periodic decluttering, simplicity
Leadership crisis	Rājarṣi-Dharma	Ethical leadership programs
Consumerism	Santoṣa (contentment)	Gratitude journaling
Identity politics	Sama-darśana (equal vision)	Inter-community education
Moral fatigue	Tapas (discipline)	Meditation, self-regulation

12 · Rebuilding from Within

When inner anarchy ends, social order begins.
The Vedas saw no difference between ecology, economy, and ethics—they are all names for harmony.
You cannot fix the world while living in internal disorder.

Each of us is a republic:

- The **mind** is our parliament—often noisy.
- The **intellect** is our judiciary—meant to discern.
- The **soul** is our constitution—eternal Dharma.

When all obey that constitution, peace returns.

13 · The Vision of Renewal

उद्भिद्यते धर्मस्य मूलं।

udbhidyate dharmasya mūlaṁ – Mahābhārata 3.206.35

Translation:
"When the root of Dharma is split, society withers."

अहिसा परमो धर्मः।

ahiṁsā paramo dharmaḥ – Mahābhārata 13.117.37

Translation:
"Non-violence is the highest Dharma."

Commentary:
Violence today isn't only physical—it's verbal, environmental, and ideological.
Revival begins with gentle speech, sustainable consumption, and inclusive thought.
The soil of Dharma revives through kindness.

14 · Closing Reflection

Reform doesn't begin in parliaments; it begins in consciousness.
When a human being becomes ethical, the ecosystem reorganises around that vibration.
When a family shares silence, the nation gains peace.
When a leader renounces greed, prosperity flows naturally.

ऋतेन देवाः पितरो नृमणा अनु।

ṛtena devāḥ pitaro nṛmaṇā anu – Rig Veda 1.164.42

"By cosmic order the gods, ancestors, and humans are sustained."

Let every action—personal, social, environmental—align with Ṛta.
That is the **Inner Republic**, where governance begins in the soul, spreads through the home, and blossoms into world harmony.

---

15 · Essence of Chapter 9

Layer	Problem	Traditional Cure	Result
Individual	Confusion, greed, burnout	Tapas, Santoṣa, Aparigraha	Inner clarity
Social	Inequality, corruption, conflict	Satya, Seva, Sama-darśana	Ethical harmony
Ecological	Waste, pollution, exploitation	Yajña, Ṛta, Bhūmi-bhakti	Sustainable order

When each citizen becomes a sādhaka, each act becomes governance, and the world becomes a temple again.

That is the rebirth of Dharma—not as dogma, but as **living rhythm**.
The **Unshakable Republic** begins with one consistent soul.

Chapter 10

The Still Center: Living the Unshakable Life

---

1 · The Whirlwind World

It's Monday morning in Mumbai. Trains thunder, inboxes bloom, timelines refresh by the second.
People rush not *toward* anything but *away* from stillness.
Rohan — a consultant who has read every productivity book —

feels both powerful and hollow.
He earns more, sleeps less, and wonders why control brings no peace.

Then one night, power cuts out.
For the first time in years, the city goes silent.
In that blackout, Rohan hears his own heartbeat.

It sounds like the drum the sages called *ṛta* — the rhythm beneath chaos.

---

2 · The Quest for Stillness

शान्तोऽहमस्मि

śānto 'ham asmi – Bṛhadāraṇyaka Upaniṣad 4.4.23

Translation: "I am peace itself."

Commentary:
Peace isn't achieved; it's remembered.

The Upaniṣadic seers didn't *create* stillness—they *recognized* it as the Self's nature.
Modern anxiety stems from outsourcing calm to circumstances.
Begin the day remembering: *Peace is what I am, not what I get.*

---

3 · Mastering Action through Equanimity

समत्वं योग उच्यते।

samatvaṁ yoga ucyate – Bhagavad Gītā 2.48

Translation: "Evenness of mind is called Yoga."

Commentary:
Success and failure, praise and blame—both are waves.
Yoga doesn't drown them; it rides them without disturbance.
Traditional Solution:
Before every major task, repeat this verse silently.
It re-centers performance in purpose, not applause.

---

4 · Right Use of Energy (Prāṇa-Śakti)

प्राणो हि सर्वं वशं आनयति।

prāṇo hi sarvaṁ vaśam ānayati – Chāndogya Upaniṣad 1.11.5

Translation: "Vital energy governs everything."

Commentary:
The ancients saw exhaustion as spiritual leakage, not workload.
Unregulated breath scatters energy; rhythmic breath re-collects it.

Practice: 2 minutes of *Sama-vṛtti Prāṇāyāma* (equal inhale/exhale) between meetings.
You'll work the same hours with half the fatigue.

---

5 · The Mirror of Speech

सत्यं वद।

satyaṁ vada – Taittirīya Upaniṣad 1.11.1

Translation: "Speak the truth."

Commentary:
In the information age, truth is rebellion.

Gossip, exaggeration, curated images—each fragment weakens integrity.
Traditional Solution: Adopt *Mauna Vrata* for ten minutes daily: silence, inner alignment, verbal detox.
Speech purified becomes mantra; life regains coherence.

---

6 · Discipline as Freedom

तपसा जायते तेजः।

tapasā jāyate tejaḥ – Atharva Veda 11.5.18

Translation: "From discipline arises radiance."

Commentary:
Modern freedom is mistaken for indulgence.
The Vedic seer knew the paradox: control intensifies joy.
Yoga, diet, timing—each small vow strengthens the spine of will.
Consistency is the new luxury.

---

7 · Compassion in an Angry Era

अहिंसा परमो धर्मः।

ahiṁsā paramo dharmaḥ – Mahābhārata 13.117.37

Translation: "Non-violence is the highest Dharma."

Commentary:
Violence today wears digital clothes—trolling, cynicism, casual cruelty.
Non-violence begins in tone.
Practice: Before posting or replying, breathe once and ask:

"Will this heal or harm?"

Softness online is modern *ahiṁsā.*

---

8 · Harmony with Nature

ऋतेन प्रथिवी स्थिताः।

ṛtena prithivī sthitāḥ – Atharva Veda 12.1.12

Translation: "The Earth stands firm through cosmic order."

Commentary:
Ecological collapse mirrors inner disorder.

Ancient India lived by *ṛta-sūkta* — seasonal balance, gratitude before use.
Solution: Restore rhythm: eat seasonal food, honour daylight, plant where you dwell.
Ritual is simply ecology performed consciously.

---

9 · The Fellowship of Souls

संगच्छध्वं संवदध्वं सं वो मनांसि जानताम्।

saṁgacchadhvaṁ saṁvadadhvaṁ saṁ vo manāṁsi jānatām – Rig Veda 10.191.2

Translation: "Move together, speak together, let your minds be one."

Commentary:
Isolation is the new poverty.
The Rig-Vedic vision of *Sangha*—community grounded in shared rhythm—heals loneliness and polarisation.
Traditional Solution: Weekly *Satsang* or circle of study;

shared chanting, shared silence.
Community built on values outlasts networking built on vanity.

---

10 · Freedom through Knowledge

तमेव वदित्वा अतमृत्युमेतिा

tameva viditvā atimṛtyum eti – Śvetāśvatara Upaniṣad 3.8

Translation: "Knowing That alone, one crosses beyond death."

Commentary:
Ignorance of Self breeds endless substitution—money for worth, applause for love, data for wisdom.
Real education ends fear.
Practice: Ten minutes of self-inquiry nightly:
"What changed today? What watched the change?"
That watcher is the immortal you.

---

11 · Traditional Dharma Solutions for Modern Problems

Modern Disorder	*Dhārmic Remedy*	*Classical Source*	*Simple Application*
Stress / Burnout	*Prāṇa-Śuddhi* – breath discipline	Chāndogya 1.11.5	3 rounds equal-breath before each task

Dishonesty / Corruption	*Satya-Vrata*	Taittirīya 1.11	Keep one small promise daily
Disconnection / Isolation	*Satsaṅga*	Rig Veda 10.191	Join value-based circles
Ecological Neglect	*Yajña-Spirit*	Atharva 12.1	Treat every act as offering
Anger / Polarisation	*Ahiṁsā*	Mahābhārata 13.117	Pause before speech
Consumerism	*Santoṣa*	Yoga Sūtra 2.42	Gratitude journal nightly
Restlessness	*Dhyāna*	Gītā 6.26	Five silent minutes morning & night
Loneliness	*Seva*	Gītā 3.19	Daily act of service
Ethical Confusion	*Viveka*	Upaniṣadic inquiry	Reflect: "Will this enlarge or shrink my awareness?"
Meaninglessness	*Ātma-Jñāna*	Śvetāśvatara 3.8	Self-study, reading, contemplation

---

12 · Rohan's Awakening

Months later, Rohan's calendar was still full, yet his mind was unhurried.
He worked, loved, and rested in the same awareness.
He had learned the secret of all ten chapters:
constancy without rigidity, engagement without entanglement.

During another blackout, he sat on his balcony watching stars return through city haze.

He whispered, *śānto 'ham asmi* — "I am peace."
This time he didn't *feel* it; he *knew* it.

---

13 · The Circle Closes

सत्येनोत्तभिता भूमिः सूर्येण तपसा धृतः।

satyenottabhitā bhūmiḥ sūryeṇa tapasā dhṛtaḥ – Atharva Veda 12.1.1

Translation: "The Earth is upheld by truth, the Sun by steadfast discipline."

Truth and discipline—*Satya* and *Tapas*—began this journey in Chapter 1 and end it here.
They are the two poles of the Unshakable life: clarity and constancy.

When you live aligned with these, work becomes worship, relationships become reflections, technology becomes tool, and stillness becomes home.

---

14 · Closing Reflection

The sages never promised a world without storms;
they promised a Self that doesn't sway.

Freedom is not absence of duty, but presence in every duty.
Peace is not withdrawal, but participation without preference.

"Be the stillness in the spin."

That is the final Dharma of consistency.

That is **Mokṣa-in-motion — the Unshakable Life.**

Chapter 11

The Return: Dharma in the Marketplace

---

1 · The Return to the World

After silence comes sound again.
When the yogi leaves the cave, the monk leaves the monastery, or the professional leaves meditation class—*that* is the true test.

Aarav, once a restless entrepreneur, has touched stillness.
Now he must bring it into boardrooms, billboards, and bazaars.
The goal is not withdrawal but **integration**—to walk among desires without being devoured by them.

---

2 · Verse 1 — The Two Paths Become One

संन्यासः कर्मयोगश्च निःश्रेयसकरावुभौ।

saṁnyāsaḥ karma-yogaś ca niḥśreyasa-karāv ubhau –

Bhagavad Gītā 5.2

Translation:

"Both renunciation and disciplined action lead to liberation."

Commentary:

The Gītā dissolves the old divide between monk and merchant. Today's world doesn't need more withdrawal; it needs awakened engagement.

Application: do your job as yoga, not escape from it—integrity replaces asceticism.

---

3 · Verse 2 — Work as Worship

कायेन मनसा बुद्ध्या केवलैरिन्द्रियैरपि।

योगिनः कर्म कुर्वन्ति सङ्गं त्यक्त्वात्मशुद्धये॥

kāyena manasā buddhyā kevalair indriyai r api |

yoginaḥ karma kurvanti saṅgaṁ tyaktvātma-śuddhaye || – BG 5.11

Translation:

"Yogis act through body, mind, and intellect—free of attachment—for inner purification."

Traditional insight:

Every profession can be tapas when done with sincerity and

detachment.

Accountability meetings become satra; emails become mantras of clarity.

---

4 · Verse 3 — The Honest Economy

असत्येन न प्रतषि्ठा।

asatyena na pratiṣṭhā – Taittirīya Upaniṣad 1.11.1

Translation:

"Without truth, nothing stands firm."

Commentary:

Modern corruption is not legal but existential—forgetting that value precedes valuation.

Solution: revive *Satya-Lakṣmī*: prosperity born of

transparency.

Ethical business isn't charity; it's the oldest profitability model.

---

5 · Verse 4 — Right Livelihood

अहसिया परमो धर्मः।

ahiṁsayā paramo dharmaḥ – Mahābhārata 13.117.37

Translation:

"Non-violence is the highest law."

Commentary:

In the global marketplace, violence hides in supply chains, exploitation, and pollution.
Solution: practise *Ahimsa-Vyāpāra*—conscious commerce: fair sourcing, ecological packaging, kindness to employees.
Profit purified becomes prayer.

---

6 · Verse 5 — Balancing Wealth and Wisdom

धर्मेण अर्थः प्रजास्यते।

dharmeṇa arthaḥ prajāsyate – Arthaśāstra 1.19

Translation:

"Wealth should be generated through Dharma."

Commentary:

Kauṭilya's principle solves modern greed.

Wealth is sacred when it circulates.
Application: donate a fixed share; support education and environment—*yajña-artham karma* in financial form.

---

7 · Verse 6 — From Competition to Contribution

लोकसंग्रहमेवापि सम्पश्यन्कर्तुमर्हसि।

loka-saṅgraham evāpi sampaśyan kartum arhasi – BG 3.20

Translation:

"Act for the maintenance of the world."

Commentary:

Individual ambition matures into collective service.

Start-ups can become *saṅgraha*—tools for community welfare.

The measure of success: how many others rise with you.

---

8 · Verse 7 — The Ecology of Time

कालो हि दुर्ग्रहम्।

kālo hi dug-graham – Mahābhārata Śānti Parva 320.42

Translation:

"Time is hard to grasp."

Commentary:

Digital multitasking has broken rhythm.

Traditional Solution: apply *Kāla-Dharma*: fixed meal hours, fixed rest, seasonal pace.
When you respect time, time respects you.

---

9 · Verse 8 — Inner Citizenship

स्वधर्मे निधनं श्रेयः परधर्मो भयावहः।

svadharme nidhanaṁ śreyaḥ para-dharmaḥ bhayāvahaḥ – BG 3.35

Translation:
"It is better to die in one's own dharma than live another's."

Commentary:
Imitation is the modern slavery.
Follow your innate duty even if humble.
Society needs excellence through authenticity, not sameness.

---

10 · Verse 9 — Stewardship of Earth

माता भूमिः पुत्रोऽहं पृथिव्याः।

mātā bhūmiḥ putro 'haṁ pṛthivyāḥ – Atharva Veda 12.1.12

Translation:
"Earth is my mother; I am her son."

Commentary:
Urban success must now re-include soil, water, and air in its profit statement.
Planting trees, supporting sustainable farming, reducing waste—these are the new rituals of citizenship.

---

11 · Verse 10 — The Still Center Amid Motion

यत्र योगेश्वरः कृष्णो यत्र पार्थो धनुर्धरः।

तत्र श्रीर्विजयो भूतिर्ध्रुवा नीतिर्मतिर्मम॥

yatra yogeśvaraḥ kṛṣṇo yatra pārtho dhanu-dharaḥ |

tatra śrīr vijayo bhūtir dhruvā nītir matir mama || – BG 18.78

Translation:
"Where there is Krishna, the Lord of Yoga, and Arjuna, the man of action, there are prosperity, victory, and stability."

Commentary:

Kṛṣṇa = awareness; Arjuna = action.

When both unite, life blossoms.
Consciousness guides activity; activity expresses

consciousness.

That is the still center in the marketplace.

---

12 · Applied Traditional Remedies

Modern Issue	Dhārmic Principle	Classical Source	Daily Application
Corrupt governance	*Satya & Śauca* (truth & purity)	Taittirīya 1.11	Transparent decision-making
Corporate exploitation	*Ahimsa*	Mahābhārata 13	Ethical sourcing & wages
Workaholism	*Kāla-Dharma*	Mahābhārata 320	Structured rest, Sabbath
Meaning crisis	*Svadharma*	BG 3.35	Purpose alignment audits
Consumer waste	*Aparigraha*	Yoga Sūtra 2.39	Minimalist lifestyle

Ecological harm	*Bhūmi-Bhakti*	Atharva 12.1	Local environmental acts
Leadership crisis	*Rājarṣi-Ideal*	Śānti Parva 88	Servant leadership programs
Community division	*Saṅgaccha dhvam*	Rig Veda 10.191	Shared projects across faiths
Cynicism	*Śraddhā*	Muṇḍaka 1.2	Renewed study & contemplation
Restlessness	*Dhyāna*	Gītā 6.26	Morning meditation

13 · Aarav's Integration

Months later, Aarav's company became India's first "Dharma-driven enterprise."

Employees meditated for five minutes before meetings; profits funded village education.

The board called it brand ethics—he knew it was karma-yoga.

He no longer sought peace away from work; he lived peace through work.

He had learned what the Gītā had whispered all along:

Renunciation is not quitting—it's quieting.

14 · The Dharma of the Future

The sages foresaw the Kali-Yuga—an age of confusion.

But they also foresaw its cure: *Smṛti-revival*, memory of sacred order.

Technology, economics, politics—all will stabilise when consciousness matures.

The next revolution is not digital—it is spiritual, powered by awareness.

नायमात्मा बलहीनेन लभ्यः।

nāyam ātmā balahīnena labhyaḥ – Muṇḍaka 3.2.4

"The Self is not for the weak."

Consistency, courage, and compassion are the three muscles of this new age.

15 · Closing Reflection — The Unshakable Vision

When the marketplace becomes monastery, when profit becomes prayer, when silence powers strategy—
then the circle of Dharma is complete.

सत्यं च धर्मं च वजियतः।

satyaṁ ca dharmaṁ ca vijayataḥ – Ṛg Veda 10.190.2

“Truth and righteousness alone triumph.”

To live the Unshakable Life is to bring sacred order into daily trade, speech, and love.

Stand steady amid speed.

Serve without self.

That is the dharma of tomorrow’s world—

The Still Center in Motion.

Chapter 12

The Heart of Harmony: Re-enchanting the Human Spirit

---

1 · A Fractured Symphony

Cities hum with engines but not with empathy.
We work beside people we never truly meet, live in high-rises that touch clouds yet rarely hearts.
The pandemic of disconnection lingers: shared screens, separate souls.

Aisha, a cultural curator, wondered why every wellness conference felt hollow.
"Where," she asked, "did the *spirit* go from our civilisation?"
The ancients would answer: the spirit left when we stopped singing together.
This chapter restores that song.

2 · Verse 1 — The Music of Oneness

सर्वं खल्विदं ब्रह्म।

sarvaṁ khalv idaṁ brahma – Chāndogya Upaniṣad 3.14.1

Translation: "All this indeed is Brahman."

Commentary:

Division is the illusion that breaks harmony.

The seer saw the same consciousness beating through bird and banker alike.

Application: daily remember: "Everything I touch is sacred."

Respect replaces rivalry.

3 · Verse 2 — Listening as Worship

श्रवणं सर्वपुण्येषु श्रेष्ठम्।

śravaṇaṁ sarva-puṇyeṣu śreṣṭham – Smṛti-saṅgraha 2.18

Translation: "Listening is the highest virtue."

Commentary:

Modern debate replaced dialogue.

The remedy is *Śravaṇa* — listening without loading a response.

In teams, homes, or politics, listening is yajña: the fire where ego burns quietly.

---

4 · Verse 3 — The Threefold Culture

वद्या ददातविनयं।

vidyā dadāti vinayaṁ – Hitopadeśa 1.1

Translation: "True learning gives humility."

Commentary:
Degrees have multiplied; wisdom has thinned.
Traditional Solution: restore *Gurukula-culture* in modern form—mentorship over management, wisdom before wealth. Schools that teach *values + skills + silence* will heal generations.

---

5 · Verse 4 — Reviving Sacred Art

यत्र नार्यस्तु पूज्यन्ते रमन्ते तत्र देवताः।

yatra nāryas tu pūjyante ramante tatra devatāḥ – Manusmṛti 3.56

Translation: "Where women are honoured, there the gods rejoice."

Commentary:
Every civilisation rises when the creative feminine is respected.
Modern relevance: honour not only women but the feminine qualities of care, intuition, and art in leadership.
Music, poetry, design — the Devi's current through culture.

---

6 · Verse 5 — Healing Loneliness through Service

परोपकाराय पुण्याय।

paropakārāya puṇyāya – Hitopadeśa 1.13

Translation: "Helping others is virtue itself."

Commentary:
Isolation ends where service begins.

Volunteerism is not charity; it's communion.
Ancient *Seva-paramparā* can rebalance digital self-fixation.
Give an hour; regain humanity.

---

7 · Verse 6 — Balancing Tradition and Innovation

नवो नित्यं नवो भवति।

navo nityaṁ navo bhavati – Ṛg Veda 8.48.3

Translation: "The eternal renews itself every moment."

Commentary:
Tradition is not museum; it's movement.
Dharma updates without uprooting.
Practice: before adopting a Western trend, ask, "What is its dhārmic equivalent?"
Fusion becomes evolution, not imitation.

---

8 · Verse 7 — The Ecology of Emotion

मैत्रीं भावय सर्वत्र।

maitrīṁ bhāvaya sarvatra – Manu 6.92

Translation: "Cultivate friendliness toward all."

Commentary:

Social media monetises outrage; sages monetised goodwill.

Traditional Remedy: *Maitrī-Bhāvanā Meditation* — repeat thrice daily, "May all beings be happy."

Neuroscience now confirms: kindness rewires the brain faster than fear.

---

9 · Verse 8 — Economy of Enough

सन्तोषात् अनुत्तमः सुखलाभः।

santoṣāt anuttamaḥ sukha-lābhaḥ – Yoga Sūtra 2.42

Translation: "From contentment arises supreme joy."

Commentary:

Consumer culture confuses comfort with happiness.

Saṁtoṣa teaches inner wealth: use what you have, give what you can.

Simplicity is civilisation's new sophistication.

---

10 · Verse 9 — The Earthly Covenant

प्राणो हि जगतः प्रतिष्ठा।

prāṇo hi jagataḥ pratiṣṭhā – Chāndogya Upaniṣad 1.11.5

Translation: "Life-breath sustains the world."

Commentary:

The ancients measured prosperity by purity of air, water, and mind.

Solution: integrate *Vedic ecology* into urban design—sacred groves, community compost, river clean-ups as modern yajña. The planet heals where gratitude replaces greed.

11 · Verse 10 —The Inner Festival

आनन्दो ब्रह्मेति व्यजानात्।

ānando brahmeti vyajānāt – Taittirīya Upaniṣad 3.6.1

Translation: "Bliss is Brahman."

Commentary:

Joy is not the reward of virtue; it is the proof of alignment. When duty and delight coincide, civilisation celebrates itself again.

Bring back shared singing, seasonal fasting, story circles—old joy technologies.

12 · Applied Dhārmic Prescriptions

Modern Crisis	Scriptural Antidote	Practical Habit
Cultural fatigue	*Vidya → Vinaya*	Mentor-led learning over degrees

Gender imbalance	*Yatra nāryas tu pūjyante*	Equal creative leadership
Loneliness	*Paropakārāya puṇyāya*	Weekly service hour
Identity conflict	*Sarvaṁ khalv idaṁ brahma*	Daily remembrance of unity
Outrage culture	*Maitrīṁ bhāvaya*	Kind-speech challenge
Consumerism	*Santoṣa*	Minimalist economy
Pollution	*Prāṇa-śuddhi*	Green breathing—trees per employee
Cultural amnesia	*Navo nityaṁ navo bhavati*	Innovate rituals, not abandon them
Meaning drought	*Ānando Brahma*	Revive art, song, celebration
Social fragmentation	*Saṅgacchadhvam saṁvadadhvam*	Create participatory festivals

13 · Aisha's Realisation

When Aisha organised the *Festival of Silence*—no mics, no selfies, just music and mindfulness—tens of thousands gathered.

No speeches, no slogans—only shared stillness.
She realised civilisation doesn't need saving; it needs remembering.
Harmony is our default frequency once noise subsides.

---

14 · Collective Renewal

Dharma isn't personal morality—it's social melody.
When individuals tune themselves, the orchestra of humanity retunes.

संगच्छध्वं संवदध्वं सं वो मनांसि जानताम्।

"Move together, speak together, let your minds be one." (Ṛg Veda 10.191.2)

That verse opened the earliest community councils and can still reopen our divided democracies.
Dialogue is the new ritual.

---

15 · Closing Reflection

Harmony is not uniformity; it is *coordinated difference.*
Just as the Vedic fire needed three logs—fuel, flame, and air—society needs three virtues:

- **Śraddhā (faith)** in goodness,
- **Seva (service)** to others, and
- **Sahṛdayatā (empathy)** toward all.

When these burn together, the dark age glows again.

धर्म एव हतो हन्ति धर्मो रक्षति रक्षितः।

dharma eva hato hanti dharma rakṣati rakṣitaḥ – Manusmṛti 8.15

Translation: "When Dharma is destroyed, it destroys; when protected, it protects."

Protect it not by slogans but by song, by kindness, by simple integrity.
That is how the **Heart of Harmony** beats again—
the sound of an *Unshakable Humanity.*

Chapter 13

The Legacy of Light: Passing the Flame of Dharma

---

1 · The Question of Continuity

When the lamp burns bright, the wise think of oil.
In an era of instant fame and forgotten values, the real challenge is not success — it's succession.

Ved, a social entrepreneur, had built an ethical company, mentored youth, and balanced profit with purpose.
But he worried: *"Will it all fade when I'm gone?"*
The ancients asked the same question. Their answer was not monuments, but *memory in motion* — the Guru–Śiṣya chain.

---

2 · Verse 1 — Knowledge as Immortality

वद्ियया अमृतमश्नुते।

vidyayā amṛtam aśnute – Īśa Upaniṣad 11

Translation: "Through knowledge one attains immortality."

Commentary:

Fame fades; wisdom flows.

Legacy is not leaving behind possessions but impressions of clarity and compassion.

Modern Practice: document experiences as teachings — blogs, mentorship, open knowledge — not for ego, but for continuity.

---

3 · Verse 2 — The Guru–Śiṣya Flame

गुरुः साक्षात् परं ब्रह्म।

guruḥ sākṣāt paraṁ brahma – Guru Gītā 17

Translation: "The Guru is verily the manifested Absolute."

Commentary:

The teacher is the human bridge of timeless truth.

When mentorship becomes transactional, knowledge dies.

Solution: re-establish mentoring as sacred trust — patience, not performance.

Teach with silence, not slides.

---

4 · Verse 3 — Lineage of Dharma

श्रुतेन तपसा ब्रह्मचर्येण शुद्धेन।

śrutena tapasā brahmacaryeṇa śuddhena – Muṇḍaka Upaniṣad 3.1.5

Translation: "By study, discipline, and purity, knowledge shines forth."

Commentary:
Transmission requires qualification.
In modern terms — integrity is bandwidth.
A polluted mind cannot carry clear truth.
Practice: digital detox before teaching, prayer before posting — keep the signal pure.

---

5 · Verse 4 — Duty to the Next Generation

पितरः पुत्रेण पालयन्ति धर्मम्।

pitaraḥ putreṇa pālayanti dharmam – Manusmṛti 2.227

Translation: "Fathers (ancestors) are protected by sons who uphold Dharma."

Commentary:

Elders live on through the values their children practice.

Solution: replace inheritance of property with inheritance of principles — storytelling dinners, family charity, shared rituals. Legacy begins at the dining table.

---

6 · Verse 5 — Words that Outlive

वाचा सत्यं ब्रूयात्।

vācā satyaṁ brūyāt – Manusmṛti 4.138

Translation: "Let one speak truth through speech."

Commentary:

Social media never dies; let your words be worthy of eternity. The Vedic seers encoded values in verses because sound carries soul.

Modern Practice: mindful communication — what you say online becomes part of the world's memory. Speak as if the future listens.

---

7 · Verse 6 — The Chain of Gratitude

नान्यं गुरुं पश्येत्।

nānyaṁ guruṁ paśyet – Guru Gītā 48

Translation: "See no one else as Guru."

Commentary:

Not exclusivity but total gratitude.

To truly receive, honour the source.

Application: begin every project by acknowledging those who taught you — citing, crediting, remembering.

Gratitude is the immune system of civilisation.

---

8 · Verse 7 — Balancing Change and Continuity

धर्मो रक्षति रक्षितः।

dharmaḥ rakṣati rakṣitaḥ – Manusmṛti 8.15

Translation: "When protected, Dharma protects."

Commentary:

To preserve Dharma is not to freeze it but to live it dynamically.

Modern reform must echo timeless principles.
Application: innovation through ethics — new technology, old conscience.

---

9 · Verse 8 — The Time-Tested Test

कालेन चाव्ययम्।

kālena cāvyayam – Gītā 10.33

Translation: "I am time, the imperishable."

Commentary:
Time judges every idea.
The test of truth: does it still bring harmony after decades?
If yes, teach it forward.
If not, evolve it through awareness.

10 · Verse 9 — Community as Custodian

संगच्छध्वं संवदध्वं सं वो मनांसि जानताम्।

saṅgacchadhvaṁ saṁvadadhvaṁ saṁ vo manāṁsi jānatām –

Rig Veda 10.191.2

Translation: "Move together, speak together, let your minds be one."

Commentary:
Legacy fails when it isolates; it thrives when it includes.
Build *satsanga networks*—interfaith, interdisciplinary, intergenerational dialogues.
Truth shared becomes timeless.

---

11 · Verse 10 — The Eternal Flame

दीपो भक्षयते ध्वान्तं कालेन भक्ष्यते स्वयं।

dīpo bhakṣayate dhvāntaṁ kālena bhakṣyate svayam –

Subhāṣita-ratna-bhāṇḍāgāra 2.21

Translation: "The lamp consumes darkness and, in time, itself."

Commentary:
Every teacher must disappear for teaching to stay.
True legacy is self-effacing light — illumination without ownership.
Practice: mentor to replace yourself, not to multiply followers.

12 · Applied Dharma for Generational Renewal

Modern Challenge	Scriptural Insight	Actionable Legacy
Loss of mentorship	*Guruḥ sākṣāt paraṁ brahma*	Create living mentor circles
Knowledge dilution	*śrutena tapasā śuddhena*	Verify before sharing; purify before posting
Family disconnection	*pitaraḥ putreṇa pālayanti dharmam*	Value storytelling & charity over inheritance
Ego-driven leadership	*dīpo bhakṣayate dhvāntam*	Serve and step aside
Cultural forgetfulness	*dharmaḥ rakṣati rakṣitaḥ*	Integrate rituals into modern formats
Misinformation	*vācā satyaṁ brūyāt*	Fact-check before speech

Intellectual arrogance	*vidyā dadāti vinayam*	Learn from multiple traditions
Burnout in activism	*kālena cāvyayam*	Act with patience, not haste
Divided societies	*saṅgacchadhvam saṁvadadhvam*	Foster value-based dialogue
Fear of death / impermanence	*vidyayā amṛtam aśnute*	Leave knowledge, not noise

---

13 · Ved's Realisation

When Ved's company celebrated its tenth anniversary, he lit a single oil lamp and passed it hand to hand through the crowd. Every person whispered a promise: to uphold truth in their sphere.
He realised immortality is not personal — it's participatory. You live on through every life you illuminate.

---

14 · Traditional Model of Continuity

Ancient India preserved truth through three pillars:

1. **Śruti** — revelation (timeless knowledge).
2. **Smṛti** — remembrance (contextual adaptation).

3. **Āchāra** — practice (living habit).

A modern civilisation can survive if it keeps these alive:

- Shruti = wisdom (science, spirituality).
- Smriti = culture (stories, values).
- Āchāra = lifestyle (sustainable living).
  When all three align, humanity regenerates like a banyan tree — branches becoming trunks.

---

15 · Closing Reflection — Light Forward

तमसो मा ज्योतिर्गमय।

tamaso mā jyotir gamaya – Bṛhadāraṇyaka 1.3.28

Translation: "Lead me from darkness to light."

We began this journey with that prayer, seeking consistency; we end with it fulfilled as continuity.
Consistency keeps life steady; continuity keeps light alive.

Dharma does not need defending; it needs demonstrating. Every act of integrity, every spark of service, every quiet correction in a corrupt system — all of it adds to the eternal lamp.

Be that lamp.

Burn clearly.

And when time comes, pass the flame.

That is how the *Unshakable Life* becomes an *Unending Light.*

Chapter 14

The Everyday Sacred: Making Life a Temple

---

1 · The Forgotten Temple

Aruna wakes at 7 a.m., reaches for her phone, scrolls, showers, sips coffee, and rushes to work.
By night, she meditates for ten minutes, feeling guilty for not doing more.

Like millions, she divides her life into "spiritual" and "practical."

But the ancients never saw two worlds.

They said: *"यददिं कञ्चि जगत् सर्वं तत्संन्यासेन भुञ्जीथा।"*

"Whatever exists in this world is to be enjoyed with renunciation." (Īśa Upaniṣad 1)

The goal isn't to escape the world, but to sanctify it.
This chapter shows how every ordinary act can become *pujā* — worship through awareness.

---

2 · Verse 1 — Seeing the Divine Everywhere

ईशावास्यमदिं सर्वं यत्कञ्चि जगत्यां जगत्।

īśāvāsyam idaṁ sarvaṁ yat kiñca jagatyāṁ jagat – Īśa Upaniṣad 1

Translation: "All this—whatever moves in the world—is pervaded by the Divine."

Commentary:

To live spiritually is to see no secular space.

Your desk, kitchen, laptop, and relationships are altars when approached with reverence.

Practice: Whisper *Namaste* in your heart before each task — acknowledging the sacred presence within it.

---

3 · Verse 2 — Work as Worship

योगः कर्मसु कौशलम्।

yogaḥ karmasu kauśalam – Bhagavad Gītā 2.50

Translation: "Yoga is excellence in action."

Commentary:

The Gītā redefined spirituality as skill in daily work.

To sweep a floor perfectly is holier than to meditate carelessly.

Modern Practice: Before beginning work, light an inner diya: say, *"May this act reflect awareness."*

Efficiency becomes devotion.

---

4 · Verse 3 — Eating as Offering

अन्नं ब्रह्मेति।

annaṁ brahmeti – Taittirīya Upaniṣad 3.2.1

Translation: "Food is Brahman."

Commentary:

Fast food, fast scrolling — the modern diet numbs sensitivity.

Ancient India treated eating as yajña — sacred exchange.

Practice: Eat in silence for one meal daily.

Chew with gratitude, seeing food as sunlight transformed.

That simple awareness transforms consumption into communion.

---

5 · Verse 4 — Speech as Prayer

वाचा सत्यम्।

vācā satyam – Taittirīya Upaniṣad 1.11.1

Translation: "Let speech be truth."

Commentary:

Every word is a vibration shaping worlds.

Unkind speech pollutes subtle space more than smoke.

Practice: Begin each day with a *mouna minute* — one minute of silence to reset verbal intention.

Speak less, mean more.

Language becomes liturgy.

6 · Verse 5 — Relationships as Mirror

आत्मनं वद्धि सिर्वत्र।

ātmānaṁ viddhi sarvatra – Mahābhārata Śānti Parva 329.12

Translation: "See your own Self in all."

Commentary:

Relationships are the clearest mirrors for ego.

When you meet irritation, see it as reflection of an inner storm.

Practice: Before reacting, pause and mentally say, *"Tat Tvam Asi" — Thou art That.*

Compassion replaces conflict.

---

7 · Verse 6 — The Discipline of Rest

न हि कश्चति क्षणमपि जातु तिष्ठत्यकर्मकृत्।

na hi kaścit kṣaṇam api jātu tiṣṭhaty akarma-kṛt – Bhagavad Gītā 3.5

Translation: "No one can remain actionless even for a moment."

Commentary:

True rest isn't absence of activity but alignment of activity with purpose.

Practice: End your day with gratitude reflection: review actions without guilt, simply observing intention.

Rest is not laziness; it's integration.

---

8 · Verse 7 — Nature as Temple

पृथिव्याः प्राणोऽहमस्मि

pṛthivyāḥ prāṇo 'ham asmi – Atharva Veda 12.1.12

Translation: "I am the breath of the Earth."

Commentary:

Ecological action is no longer optional; it's spiritual hygiene. Planting, composting, conserving — these are forms of modern *homa* (sacrifice).

Practice: Keep one living plant in every workspace.

Tend it as you tend awareness.

Green is the colour of gratitude.

---

9 · Verse 8 — Technology as Tool of Dharma

कर्मणि व्यापृतो ह्ययम् आत्मा।

karmaṇi vyāpto hy ayam ātmā – Gītā Bhāṣya (Śaṅkara)

Translation: "The Self pervades action."

Commentary:

Technology can either distract or divine.

It depends on intent.

Use screens to learn, teach, and connect — not to escape.

Traditional Principle: *Yajña* means "that which unites through offering."

Let your online time become a digital yajña — an offering of value, not vanity.

---

10 · Verse 9 — The Power of Small Rituals

नित्यं यज्ञः।

nityaṁ yajñaḥ – Smṛti-sāra 5.8

Translation: "Daily sacrifice sustains life."

Commentary:

Ritual isn't superstition; it's structure for consciousness.

Five minutes of prayer, one candle, one mindful breath — these keep the invisible current flowing.

Practice: Micro-ritualize your life:

- Morning: gratitude to sun.
- Noon: moment of silence before food.
- Night: forgiveness reflection.

  Three acts anchor the day.

---

11 · Verse 10 — The Inner Sanctum

अन्तर्बहिश्च तत्सर्वं व्याप्य नारायणः स्थितिः।

antar bahiś ca tat sarvaṁ vyāpya nārāyaṇaḥ sthitaḥ –

Nārāyaṇa Sūkta 5

Translation: "Within and without, all is pervaded by the Divine."

Commentary:

The temple is not a place; it is perception.

When awareness becomes steady, even traffic lights glow with sanctity.

Practice: At least once daily, pause in public and silently remember: *"This too is sacred."*

That moment redeems the whole day.

---

12 · The Sacred Integration Table

Aspect of Modern Life	Dhārmic Lens	Practice
Work	*Karma-Yoga*	Offer effort, drop ego
Family	*Seva*	Serve without demand
Food	*Yajña*	Eat with gratitude
Technology	*Upāsanā*	Use as learning & sharing

Money	*Artha–Dharma*	Earn ethically, spend usefully
Rest	*Prāṇa–Saṁyam*	Mindful breathing before sleep
Relationships	*Bhakti*	See Divine in others
Speech	*Satyam–Mauna*	Truth + Silence
Nature	*Bhūmi–Pūjā*	Plant, protect, participate
Time	*Kāla–Ārādhana*	Honour sunrise, sunset rhythms

13 · Aruna's Realisation

Six months later, Aruna's routine looked the same — laptop, commute, deadlines.

But her *perception* had changed.

She bowed inwardly before logging in, blessed her lunch, smiled at her inbox as if it were scripture.

Her friends said she'd become peaceful without reason.

She called it: *Living the Temple.*

---

14 · Everyday Sacredness in Society

When one person sanctifies daily life, families regain grace.
When families practice reverence, communities regain trust.
When nations live by sacred rhythm, the planet heals.

ऋतेन देवाः पितिरो नृमणा अनु।

ṛtena devāḥ pitaro nṛmaṇā anu – Ṛg Veda 1.164.42

Translation: "By cosmic order the gods, ancestors, and humans are sustained."

Order begins in one heartbeat aware of its holiness.

---

15 · Closing Reflection — The Unshakable Temple

The Vedas never built a single cathedral of stone; they built consciousness into conduct.
You are that temple.
Every breath is incense, every act an offering, every thought a mantra.

तत्त्वमसि।

tat tvam asi – Chāndogya 6.8.7

Translation: “Thou art That.”

When you live this truth, life stops being a struggle and becomes a sacred ceremony.
The world doesn’t need more religion; it needs more *reverence.*
And reverence begins with consistency —
the rhythm of remembrance that turns the ordinary into the divine.

That is the final stage of the *Unshakable Life* —
not withdrawal, not worship,
but **awakening in action.**

Epilogue

The Unshakable Light: Beyond Time and Thought

---

1 · The Silence After the Last Word

When the scriptures end, silence begins.
After the final verse, when ink dries and lamps dim, what

remains is not knowledge, but knowing.It is that soft awareness which doesn't need to remember; it simply *is*.

You have travelled through the ten thousand moods of life — action and stillness, joy and fatigue, success and surrender.Now, the path bends inward — not to renounce the world, but to see it rightly.In that seeing, the journey completes itself.

---

2 · The Lamp Within

दीपो भक्षयते ध्वान्तं कालेन भक्ष्यते स्वयं।

dīpo bhakṣayate dhvāntaṁ kālena bhakṣyate svayam –

Subhāṣita Ratna Bhāṇḍāgāra 2.21

"The lamp dispels darkness, and in time, is consumed itself."

All wisdom traditions agree: the true teacher burns to give light. So does the sincere seeker.
Consistency is not endless repetition; it is the devotion to keep burning without demand for reward.
You are both lamp and flame.

Let this book, too, burn out — so that its essence may glow quietly inside you.

---

3 · The Rhythm of Being

There is a pulse beneath thought — a silence that hums even in noise.
That is your *Ātman*, the unshakable witness.

अजो नित्यः शाश्वतोऽयं पुराणो न हन्यते हन्यमाने शरीरे।

ajo nityaḥ śāśvato’yaṁ purāṇo na hanyate hanyamāne śarīre –

Bhagavad Gītā 2.20

“Unborn, eternal, ancient, the Self is not slain when the body is slain.”

This verse is no abstraction; it’s direct instruction.
When you act from this awareness, no situation can destroy your peace.
You can love without clinging, work without fear, lead without pride.
The unshakable one is not cold; he is completely alive — yet untouched.

---

4 · The Final Lesson of Consistency

At the start, you sought *discipline*; now you discover *rhythm.*
Discipline is will imposed on time.
Rhythm is will aligned with time.

The Gītā whispered it all along:

कर्मण्येवाधिकारस्ते मा फलेषु कदाचन।

karmaṇy-evādhikāras te mā phaleṣu kadācana – BG 2.47

Freedom was never the absence of effort; it was the absence of anxiety.
Work will continue.
The wise simply work without wobble.
They are rivers flowing, not reservoirs straining.

---

5 · The Three Jewels Remembered

In the *Unshakable* journey, you met three eternal principles — the same thread that runs through every Upaniṣad and heart:

1. **Satya — Truth:** the courage to see things as they are.
2. **Śraddhā — Faith:** the trust that what is real cannot be lost.

3. **Santoṣa — Contentment:** the serenity of enoughness.

When these three dance together, even chaos becomes choreography.

---

6 · The World as Teacher

Every traffic jam, heartbreak, failure, and friendship — each has been a scripture in disguise.
You don't need another guru; life itself instructs, if you listen without hurry.

उत्तिष्ठत जाग्रत प्राप्य वरान्निबोधत।

uttiṣṭhata jāgrata prāpya varān nibodhata – Kaṭha Upaniṣad 1.3.14

"Arise, awake, and learn from the wise."

Rise daily, not just from bed but from forgetfulness.
Awaken, not from sleep but from the trance of busyness.
Learn, not to collect knowledge but to polish presence.

---

7 · Beyond Belief, Into Being

Philosophy ends where perception begins.
Truth is not an opinion to hold but a clarity to inhabit.
When seen rightly, even contradiction harmonizes.

एको देवः सर्वभूतेषु गूढः सर्वव्यापी सर्वभूतान्तरात्मा।

eko devaḥ sarva-bhūteṣu gūḍhaḥ sarva-vyāpī sarva-bhūtāntar-ātmā – Śvetāśvatara Upaniṣad 6.11

"The One Divine, hidden in all beings, is the inner Self of all."

This is the final dharma — not moral, but metaphysical:
to see the One in all, and to act accordingly.

---

8 · Modern Mokṣa

Liberation in our age is not found in caves or Himalayas.
It is found in a clear mind during a meeting, in gentleness amid argument, in calm scrolling through chaos.

Mokṣa today means **awareness unbroken by distraction.**

That is why the sages called it *Nirvāṇa* — not disappearance, but coolness.

When the fire of craving is quenched, the same flame becomes light.

यदा विनियतं चित्तमात्मन्येवावतिष्ठते।

yadā viniyataṁ cittam ātmany evāvatiṣṭhate – BG 6.18

"When the controlled mind rests in the Self, one is said to be in Yoga."

---

9 · The Four Gifts to Carry Forward

Gift	Essence	Modern Application
Śravaṇa (Listening)	Receive truth humbly	Read and reflect daily, not reactively
Manana (Reflection)	Question until it settles	Journal your insights
Nididhyāsana (Absorption)	Live the truth	Turn routines into rituals
Sevā (Service)	Give it away	Mentor, teach, serve silently

The highest knowledge is proven only when shared in silence through action.

10 · The Circle of Fire

Everything ends where it began:
A spark became a flame, a flame became fire, fire became light.

Now the light rests in you.
Let it move through your words, your work, your warmth.
Be consistent not for perfection, but for remembrance.

तमेव वदित्िवा अतमिृत्युमेति।

tameva viditvā atimṛtyum eti – Śvetāśvatara Upaniṣad 3.8

"Knowing That alone, one goes beyond death."

Knowledge doesn't conquer death; it dissolves its relevance.
Time continues, but you—awareness—remain untouched.

11 · Gratitude and Return

The author bows here — not to an audience, but to Existence itself.
Every verse quoted, every story told, is borrowed from a continuum older than memory.

The words may fade, but their fragrance lingers wherever sincerity abides.

Let these pages return you not to doctrines, but to *your own experience* —
to the still pulse beneath your name and narrative.

---

12 · The Closing Verse

ओं पूर्णमदः पूर्णमदिं पूर्णात् पूर्णमुदच्यते।

पूर्णस्य पूर्णमादाय पूर्णमेवावशिष्यते॥

oṁ pūrṇam adaḥ pūrṇam idaṁ pūrṇāt pūrṇam udacyate |

pūrṇasya pūrṇam ādāya pūrṇam evāvaśiṣyate – Īśa Upaniṣad Invocation

Translation:
"That is Whole, this is Whole.
From the Whole the Whole arises.
When the Whole is taken from the Whole, the Whole remains."

Commentary:
You began this journey seeking completeness.
You end it discovering: you were never incomplete.

Everything that flows from the Whole remains whole —
including you.

---

13 · Final Reflection — The Unshakable Light

The world will keep spinning faster.
New distractions will arise, new storms will come.
But within you, the ancient rhythm continues — calm, luminous, untouched.

That rhythm is not something to maintain — it maintains *you.*
It is your **Unshakable Light.**

May you walk with that light —
not as seeker or preacher,
but as presence itself.

Let your life whisper softly,
as the sages once did:

शान्तिः शान्तिः शान्तिः॥

śāntiḥ śāntiḥ śāntiḥ

Peace, Peace, Peace.

Author's Note

If this book touched you, don't quote it — live it.

Let consistency become compassion,

discipline become devotion,

and success become serenity.

Then you, too, will join the timeless lineage of

those who kept the flame alive —

the silent saints of everyday life.

You are the Unshakable Light.

www.ingramcontent.com/pod-product-compliance
Lightning Source LLC
Chambersburg PA
CBHW062138160726
48282CB00027B/864
9789334456691